Executive Marbles
& Other Team Building Activities

Sam Sikes

Copyright© 1998 by Sam Sikes
ISBN   0-9646541-2-1

Learning Unlimited Corporation
5155 East 51st, Suite 108
Tulsa, OK 74135
(918) 622-3292   fax (918) 622-4203
Printed in the United States of America

Table of Contents

Acknowledgements

A sincere thank you goes to the people who made this book possible and the organizations they represent.

Thank you Clear Channel Communications, AmeriCorps, University of Tulsa, NYLC, Amoco, Town & Country Schools, and State Farm teams and friends for allowing us to take your pictures and publish them.

A special thanks goes to my wife Sara for putting up with the intensity of me writing another book, my business partners Mary and Glen for taking up the slack as the book was under construction, and my dad who helped with the editing.

Disclaimer

All activities contain some inherent risk of injury whether it be physical or emotional. The author has devoted reasonable attention to the safety of any activity included within this book by describing potential hazards and testing the activities with others.

The reader assumes all risk and liability for any loss or damage that may result from the use of the materials contained in this book. Liability for any claim, whether based upon errors or omissions in this book shall be limited to the purchase price of this book.

Matrix Of Recommended Team Sizes

(*) One facilitator can manage multiple teams

Number In Team	2-5	6-10	11-15	16-20	21-30	30+
*6-Count		x	x	x	x	x
Alignment Lift		x	x	x	x	
*Balloon Foosball					x	x
Big Event					x	x
*Bolt In A Bottle	x	x	x	x		
*Captain Is Coming				x	x	x
*Capture The Rope			x	x	x	
*Champs Or Chumps			x	x	x	
Command Performance			x	x	x	
*Communalities					x	x
*Creative Mind Benders	x	x	x	x		
*Cubicles			x	x	x	
*Executive Marbles	x					
Flying Squirrel		x	x			
*Hot Air Balloons	x	x				
*Identity Crisis			x	x	x	
*Insanity				x	x	x
*Juggling		x	x	x	x	x
*Knowledge Is Power	x					
Masking Tape Ideas		x	x	x		
Mouse Trap	x					
*OD = E2		x	x	x		
*Onimod		x	x	x	x	
*Paper Chute	x	x				
*Partner Stretches	x	x	x	x	x	x
*Phone Tag		x	x	x	x	
Portable Islands		x	x			
*Quadrapus		x	x	x		
Rock Paper Scissors		x	x	x	x	

Recommended Team Sizes cont. . .
(*) One facilitator can manage multiple teams

Number In Team	2-5	6-10	11-15	16-20	21-30	30+
*Thinking Outside Box			x	x	x	x
*Tick					x	x
Urban Zip			x	x		
*Water Towers	x	x				
*Water Fall	x	x	x			
*Work, Rest & Play Mate	x					

Issues and Concepts

T   -   Trust
C   -   Communication
L   -   Leadership
R R   -   Roles and Responsibilities
D   -   Direction
P I   -   Process Improvement
E   -   Energizers
P S   -   Problem Solving
CM   -   Conflict Management
CR   -   Creativity
K   -   Know Others Better
CC   -   Competition/Cooperation
F   -   Fun

6-Count   -   C, F
Alignment Lift   -   L, D
Balloon Foosball   -   E, CC, F
Big Event   -   T, C, L, RR, PS, CM, CC
Bolt In A Bottle   -   PS, CR
Captain Is Coming   -   E, F
Capture The Rope   -   E, PS, CC, F
Champs Or Chumps   -   C, PS, CC
Command Performance   -   C, E, F
Communalities   -   C, K
Creative Mind Benders   -   PS, CR
Cubicals   -   C, L, RR, PI, E, CC, F
Executive Marbles   -   T, C, L, RR, PS, CC, F
Flying Squirrel   -   T, F
Hot Air Balloons   -   C, L, RR, PS, CR, F
Identity Crisis   -   C, L, RR, D, PI, CM, CC
Insanity   -   C, L, CM, CR, CC
Juggling   -   C, PI, E, K, F
Knowledge Is Power   -   PS
Mouse Trap   -   C, L, RR, PS, CR
OD=E^2 -   C, L, RR, D, PS, CM, CC
Onimod   -   C, L, E, PS, K, F
Paper Chute   -   L, RR, PI, PS, CR

Issues and Concepts cont. . .

Introduction

Hello Again!

Three years ago I wrote a book similar to this one called *Feeding The Zircon Gorilla*. Like *Executive Marbles*, it took its name from one of the activities within the book. The activities in both books were created for actual teams and customized for the various needs of many customers. The book is written for the adult learner; however, facilitators who work with children and teens have enjoyed most of the activities by making minor modifications to the instructions (no pun intended).

One of the main reasons for writing this book is to add new activities into the growing field of experiential training. Many activities in newer publications are recycled or simply conversational. I recently opened an envelop advertising a free experiential activity inside. When I read the instructions, I realized the "experiential activity" was a simple brainstorm and set of questions. By experiential in this book I mean that people are put into dynamic situations similar to their actual work environments to practice and develop skills. I ask people to look, feel, and listen to themselves and the people around them as they participate in an activity. What was successful? What could have been improved? Keep what works and avoid what does not. It is learning through experience.

There are many ways people learn. Some of the more standard categories include visual, auditory, and tactile. People do have learning preferences. Experiential learning is the most powerful way I have ever seen to change behavior and change attitudes. The speed at which the feedback kicks you in the pants or lifts your spirits is hard to beat. People get immediate feedback on how well they accomplish

1

tasks. Following closely behind, they get interpersonal feedback in the areas of trust, conflict, behavioral style, and leadership, to name a few.

What I have not emphasized in this book are the questions a facilitator should ask before, during, and after the activities. The art and science of processing the experience is vital to the success of experiential methods of training, but it is beyond the scope and purpose of this book.

Getting The Most Out Of This Book

One of the first things you may notice about the book is the animated cartoon at the bottom of the odd numbered pages. Just start at the front of the book and flip through the pictures to get the effect. It's just for fun!

The book is organized so that you can find the information you need quickly. The activities are arranged in alphabetical order. Once you know the name of an activity, you will have no problem locating it. The table of contents lists all the major sections including the "extras" I have scattered among the activities. Extras are interesting stories or information related to facilitating activities. The extra text and picture sections are marked by a "•" in the table of contents.

Each activity has been divided into headings such as "PREPARATION" so that each activity is easier to understand. Each activity starts with a photograph. Diagrams and other drawings and pictures are included to help explain the instructions. At the end of several activities I have listed some ideas for variations that we have used successfully in our training.

Immediately following the table of contents are two reference pages for facilitator planning purposes. I received requests to add these after the Gorilla book. One gives information about how many people can best experience each activity. It also indicates whether or not the activity can be facilitated by one facilitator and many groups or if there should be one facilitator for each group. The other page lists what learning objectives tend to stand out for each activity. The list of objectives includes several of the more common topics that the activities bring to life.

I converted the measurements in each "PROPS" heading to both English and metric. Too many people around the world use the metric system not to add the conversions.

Finally, I included information about our other resources at the end of the book. As you have success stories and variations to share, give us a call. It is always a thrill to hear how people enjoy themselves and learn at the same time.

Enjoy the experience!

6-Count

6-Count

PROPS:
None

OBJECTIVE:
This is a good, quick icebreaker that stretches people's minds and smile muscles.

HISTORY:
John Irvin taught me this activity several years ago. He had found it in some research to exercise left and right brain activity.

PREPARATION:
The only real preparation you must do before this activity is practice going through the movements. Be sure you can do them slowly and quickly without thinking too carefully about the movements.

INSTRUCTIONS:
Does anyone know how to do a 6-count? It goes 1, 2, 3, 4, 5, 6.

Count from 1 to 6 with everyone at the same time. (Do it again with "feeling".)

Put movement to the count by raising your left hand above your head and down to your side. Your hand should go up on 1, 3, and 5 and down on 2, 4, and 6. (Repeat with feeling.)

Give your left arm a rest and let's give a movement to your right arm. It goes up on 1, straight out to the side on 2, down on 3, up on 4, straight out to the side on 5, down on 6. It makes the shape of a triangle. (Repeat with feeling.)

Now, as if you hadn't guessed, we will put both the arm actions together with the count. Your left arm still goes up and down while your right arm still goes up out and down. (You might want to go fairly slowly, but don't expect many people to get it right.)

FACILITATOR NOTES:
This is a good activity to follow physical stretching. The 6-count actually stretches the brain and the voice.

Don't take much time with the activity. Keep it moving and stay in control of the group. I have noticed that it helps the group hear instructions better after the 6-count possibly because it gets everyone focused on accomplishing the same task at the same time.

Alignment Lift

Alignment Lift

PROPS:
- 2 pieces of 11 mm nylon climbing rope 30-50 feet (9.15-15.24 m) long
- 2 carabiners
- 1 rope pulley
- 10 feet (3 m) nylon webbing or 11 mm nylon climbing rope

OBJECTIVE:
Demonstrate the value of goal alignment and lift a person off the ground.

HISTORY:
I was listening to a speaker talk about corporate alignment when I "heard" a concept that I had to write down. Alignment is not only about getting everyone to go in the same direction. Alignment is getting people to go toward a common goal. It is a subtle difference in many cases, yet I thought it was significant at the time. After much thought about how to illustrate the alignment idea I looked to my ropes course experience and made the Alignment Lift.

PREPARATION:
You will be lifting a person off the ground. Use strong knots that will hold the weight of at least one person without coming apart. I would suggest a bowline and a double fisherman's knot.

Locate a large tree limb, pipe or beam 8-12 feet off the ground. Tie the webbing or short rope securely around the limb and attach the pulley using a carabiner.

Thread one long rope through the pulley. Tie a secure loop in one end approximately 3 feet in diameter for a person to sit in

and a small secure loop in the other to connect the two ropes.

Tie the second long rope into a circle and join the two ropes with a carabiner.

Decide who or what the group will lift. A heavier person or object will make a more dramatic result.

INSTRUCTIONS:

Phase I - Misalignment
1) Everyone grab hold of the rope and stand in a loose circle inside the rope.
2) Close your eyes and and turn your bodies to face North as best you can.
3) Open your eyes, point straight ahead, and walk straight in the direction you just pointed while holding the rope. You are trying to lift the person at the end of the rope off the ground.

Notice how effective you were. What were your barriers?

Phase II - Same direction, different destination
1) Everyone get back into your original circle and watch as I point North.
2) Now that you know which direction is North, point to something exactly North of you and walk straight North while pulling on the rope. Do not move in any direction but North. Try to stay in your circle. Stop before the person goes through the pulley.
3) (If applicable) Lower the person slowly.

Notice how effective you were. What were your barriers that time?

Phase III - Same direction, same destination
1) Stay inside the rope still holding it and form single file line pointing North. The first person in line will

be farthest north and the last person in line will be farthest south.
2) Now carefully walk straight North and stop before the person goes through the pulley.
3) Lower the person slowly.

Notice how effective you were. What were some differences between this last time and the times before?

FACILITATOR NOTES:

This activity does not take too long to facilitate. It is less of a problem solving opportunity and more of an active demonstration. A group can do the activity easily with as few as 5 lifters. If you have more than 20 lifters, lift 2 people or a heavier weight.

During Phase III, be aware of the people at the front of the line. Sometimes people toward the back of the line will push on the people in front of them rather than pulling on the rope. The people in the front can get squashed.

No part of this activity is designed to go too quickly.

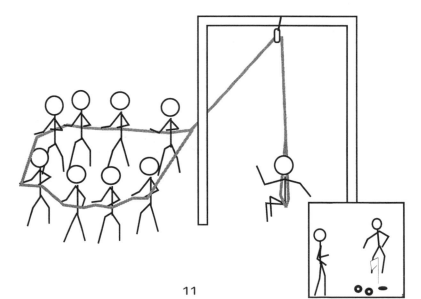

Balloon Foosball (4-Way)

Balloon Foosball (4-Way)

PROPS:
- Four equal numbers of four colors of balloons
- Goal line markers (rope, cones, masking tape, etc.)
- 8 or more large clear plastic trash bags

OBJECTIVE:
Teams try to bat their balloons to their team's goal so that "stuffers" can place their team's balloons in a bag. The team with the most bagged balloons wins.

HISTORY:
A person called our office one day. She was frantically searching for an activity to deliver to a crowd of 800 people. It had to be 1) Fun, 2) Meaningful, and 3) No more than 10 minutes long. It was quite a request, so we put our heads together and created Balloon Foosball. We have tried it many times with large groups and it is always a great activity for photograph or video.

PREPARATION:
Gather four colors of balloons enough for at least one per person and mix them in a container so that the colors are random (additional rounds will require more balloons).

Ask for volunteers to help answer questions and provide assistance to the facilitator during the activity.

Place the goal boundaries in four separate areas of the room. Put some clear plastic bags in each goal area. A flip chart page taped to the wall at each goal area works well to tell which colors goes where.

For large groups, a speaker system will be

necessary to communicate to the whole group. Write the basic instructions on a large overhead projector or several flip charts.

Prepare to start and stop the group with a whistle or shout of some sort.

Facilitating a quick stretch and a brief mention of safety concerns would be a good idea.

INSTRUCTIONS:

Ask the whole group to spread themselves around the game area so that they all have enough room around them to move freely without bumping each other.

Select one or two people for each of the four goal areas and send them to their areas.

Announce the following instructions:

Stay where you are. A person with colored balloons will be approaching you. Take the balloons and equally distribute them so that everyone has one balloon. Everyone should blow up his balloon(s).

You now should have one inflated balloon in your hand. The balloon's color determines which team you are on.

In just a minute I will ask you to move your balloons toward your "team's" goal while keeping other balloons away from the other team's goals. Inside your goal area you will need a few "stuffers" to stuff your team's inflated balloons into bags. You must hit balloons into the air, not hand them to another person.

There are two team roles:

Movers can hit any balloons; however, movers cannot walk around the room. They can only pivot on one foot like in basketball. No movers can be in a goal area. Balloons must be batted to another person, not handed off.

Stuffers put their team's balloons into clear plastic bags. Stuffers cannot leave the goal area.

After a designated amount of time (for example, 2 minutes) the game facilitator will signal a stop to end the game. All activity must stop when I sound the signal. Each team's stuffers should total the team's points then.

Scoring
A team scores a point for every <u>inflated balloon</u> that the stuffers have stuffed into a bag. Deduct a point for every balloon in the goal area that is from another team.

If there is time for another round, ask the whole group to take 30 seconds to pop all the balloons and pass the balloon skins to a trash bag at any of the four goal areas. Once the balloons are gone, start another round.

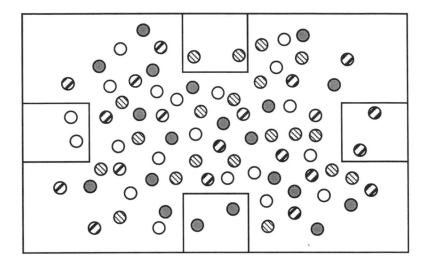

FACILITATOR NOTES:

For the most part, this activity is designed to make a big visual impact. It wakes people up and is fun. It is a quick activity, so be prepared to move on to another round or transition into your next agenda item.

Remember that many people are color blind. Avoid using blue and green balloons together. Also avoid choosing the tiny 3 to 6-inch balloons. Many people have trouble inflating them and they fall to the ground too quickly. I prefer the 9-inch balloons you can find at most hobby stores.

VARIATIONS:

If you have fewer than 60 people, consider using only three goal areas and three balloon colors.

To change the game to a more strategic tone, ask everyone to get five balloons of the same color, but only inflate one for each round. At the end of each round, allow everyone to move just one step in any direction before starting the next round. The strategic planning is individualized and uncoordinated unless someone from a team reveals the ideas to the entire group.

The Big Event

The Big Event

PROPS:
The following items will vary depending on what activities you use and how many people you have in the group. Gather these props for the Big Event below.

- 1-3 sets of Trolleys or Team Skis
- 20 Marshmallow or Acid River boards [scrap lumber pieces varying from 4 inches to 1 foot (10-30.5 cm) long]
- 15 outside corner moldings about 2 feet (61 cm) long and 1 marble for Gutterball
- Several tennis balls or other "mines" for Mine Field
- 10 blindfolds for Mine Field
- 1 long rope for Mine Field border
- 200-300 feet (61-91 m) of string for the 3-D Spider Web
- Instruction sheets for each team
- Tape or tacks to attach the instructions to the starting places
- 8 hula hoops

OBJECTIVE:
Several teams move interdependently through three initiatives while maximizing profits and minimizing costly mistakes.

HISTORY:
Many companies we work with use a team-based work structure. One of the difficulties with having several teams is that each needs to coordinate with the others to some extent. We enjoy crossover events where a team starts a here-to-there activity at one end and another team starts at the other end, so we expanded upon that idea with the Big Event. The challenges of coordination and communication stand out in this activity.

PREPARATION:

Take time to describe the whole activity to all the facilitators so that you minimize confusion. There will be a lot of action happening at the same time when the Big Event begins.

Look at the map of the event and lay out all the equipment and supplies ahead of time. Each starting hoop should have the Big Event Introduction, the IntraNet instructions, and the instructions for their particular starting event. Do not give the instructions to any other group's starting event.

Consider preparing water or other drinks for the participants since this often takes 2 hours to complete.

INSTRUCTIONS:

You are all part of one organization yet you have different jobs within the business. You will be starting a journey with your team that will take you through three distinct challenges. Read the instructions carefully at the beginning of your journey and take full advantage of the resources within your team.

A facilitator will stay with each team and help clarify questions. I would suggest that at least one person from your team serve as an accountant for your budget.

FACILITATOR NOTES:

You can substitute the activities described in these instructions with your favorite activities. The activities need to be here-to-there activities and take approximately the same amount of time to solve.

"Okay everyone, stand in a circle, turn to the person on your right and shake hands." What happens? You try to shake hands, but you cannot because the person to your right needs a hand from someone else. People have the same reaction during the Big Event. Because the Big Event is interconnected, no one team finishes long before another. For example, the team starting at the Marshmallows must wait to get instructions about the Trolleys from the team that started at the Trolleys. At the same time, the Trolley team needs information about the Mine Field from the other team. A curious dynamic occurs. The teams are not in a two-way information exchange. They need to tell one team what they know, but they need to ask for information from another team.

You will need a facilitator for each team. The facilitator should stay with the same team throughout the event so that the processing afterwards can be specific and applicable to each team. I would suggest that each small team create a list of "lessons learned" to present to the large group after the small group discussions.

VARIATIONS:

The number of small teams and the number of different activities can vary depending on how many people you have or how large you want each team. Three small teams and five small teams both work well.

The Big Event Introduction
It begins. . .

As soon as possible, everyone stand with at least one foot in the hula hoop before reading the rest of this message. This message must stay at this location. (You cannot take it with you.)

The hoops must stay where they are, but as long as a person has at least one foot in a hoop, he or she can make no costly "mistakes".

Success in business is ensured by doing the right things and having a little luck along the way. In the same way, missing opportunities and making mistakes costs you. Your company is no exception. Finding, creating, and maintaining business is paramount to continued success.

Today, and today only, you have the opportunity to gain or lose new income from your services. Your small team has a budget of $1 million to make the journey from where you are to where you need to finish.

Your team's journey is 1) from this hoop to the hoop at the IntraNet, 2) through the Net to the hoop on the left, then 3) to the other team's hoop where they are starting now (clockwise from where you now stand). You have the instructions for safely reaching the Net and getting through the net. You will have to get the information you need for the last leg of your journey from another team.

IntraNet Instructions
(Common Company Communications Center)

The IntraNet is the only location where you may communicate with other teams. <u>Terrible</u> consequences may occur if your team tries to communicate with other teams while outside the Net.

Crossing the distance from the hoop near the Net to the hoop across the Net without making <u>any</u> mistakes will gain your team $1 million.

Touching or disturbing the Net once your feet are out of a hoop will cost you $100,000 for each mistake. And yes, the supports on which the net is tied <u>are</u> part of the net.   No one may intentionally alter the Net.

(You will need to communicate with others to discover how to cross the third leg of your journey without mistakes.)

Good Luck!!!!!

Trolleys

You may have noticed the boards with ropes attached to them. These are your travel resources from the hoop where you are now to the next hoop at the Net. Once you enter the Net, you will no longer need the trolleys.

Crossing the distance from this hoop to the one at the Net without making any mistakes will gain you $1 million.

Touching the ground from hoop to hoop with anything except the boards will cost you $100,000 each time it occurs and may have other consequences.

• •

Marshmallows

You may have noticed the blocks on the ground near you. These are your travel resources from the hoop where you are now to the next hoop at the Net. Everyone must be out of your starting hoop before anyone can enter the hoop at the Net. Once you enter the Net, you will no longer need the marshmallows (blocks) so just leave them at the entrance.

The number of blocks you may take on your journey is one per person on your team minus one. For example, if you have 15 people, you can take 14 blocks on your trip. Once the journey has begun, if you lose physical contact with a block it will be considered an unneeded resource and the facilitator will take it away.

Crossing the distance from this hoop to the one at the Net without making any mistakes will gain you $1 million.

Touching the ground from hoop to hoop with
anything except the blocks will cost you $100,000
each time it occurs and may have other consequences.

••

Mine Field

You may have noticed the items (balls) on the
ground near you surrounded by a boundary. Think of
these items as mistakes and obstacles waiting to
happen. The boundary is a guide to let you know
where you may travel from the hoop where you are
now to the next hoop at the Net. When you travel
outside the hoop you will need to completely cover
your eyes with a bandanna and stay within the
boundary.

Once you reach the hoop at the Net, you will no
longer need the bandannas.

Each person who crosses the distance from this hoop
to the hoop at the Net without making any mistakes
gains your company $100,000.

Touching an item (a mine) with anything or stepping
outside the boundary from hoop to hoop will cause
the person who touched or stepped out to have to
start over (costing your team time). Terrible things
will happen if travelers' eyes are not covered.

••

Gutterball

You may have noticed the gutters and ball near your
hoop. These are your travel resources from the hoop
where you are now to the next hoop at the Net.
Once you reach the Net, you will no longer
need the gutters or the ball. Leave the
resources in the hoop at the Net.

25

Rulz:

A person with the ball cannot move his or her feet. If you drop the ball to the ground, the whole team must begin again from the starting hoop. A different person must hold each gutter and his or her own pinkies must stay in contact with each other while they have the ball in the gutter.

The ball must travel on each gutter in sequence before contacting the first gutter again.

Crossing the distance from this hoop to the one at the Net without making <u>any</u> mistakes will gain you $1 million.

The following mistakes will cost you $100,000 each time one occurs:
• The ball is dropped
• The ball is transported without pinkies touching
• Gutters touch each other
• The ball touches anything except a gutter during transportation

Big Event Map

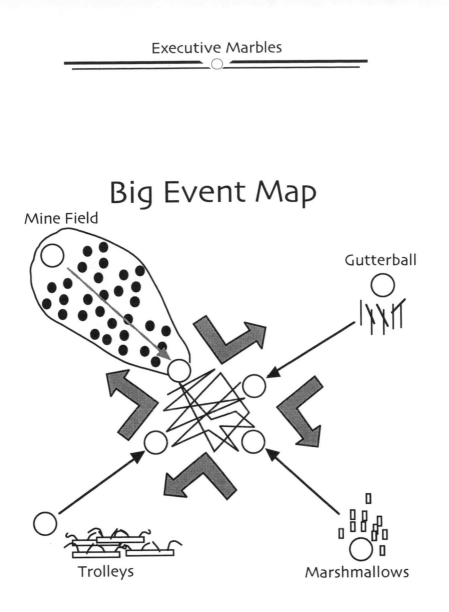

Mine Field

Gutterball

Trolleys

Marshmallows

Bolt in a Bottle

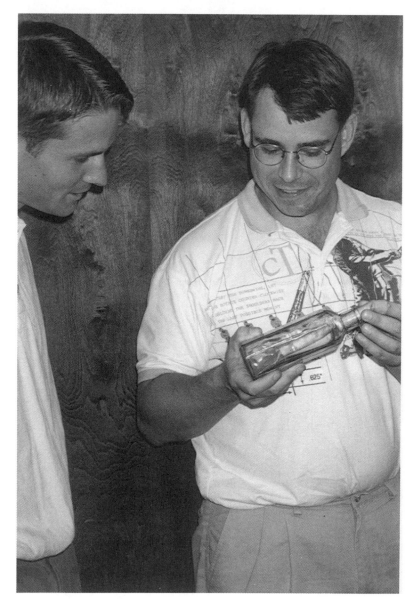

Bolt in a Bottle

PROPS:

- A bottle (glass vinegar bottles work well)
- 1 dowel rod with a diameter slightly smaller than the bottle opening and as long as the bottle
- 1 machine bolt and matching nut

Many types of nuts, bolts, rods, and bottles work. Here are the specifics I often use: a 1 pint (473 ml) vinegar bottle, 5/8 inch (16 mm) dowel rod approximately 6 3/4 inches (17.15 cm) long, a 1/4 inch (6.4 mm) diameter bolt 1 1/2 inches (38 mm) long

OBJECTIVE:

Unscrew the nut and remove the dowel rod from the bottle.

HISTORY:

I first heard about this impossible puzzle three years ago after discussing a similar puzzle with Cappy Leland. It is not a puzzle I have seen many times so I wanted to share it.

PREPARATION:

You will need to assemble the puzzle before someone can take it apart. I would say that you could make the assembly part of the original presentation to people, but the motivation to undo the impossible has seemed greater for people than creating the impossible.

See page 206 for the secret instructions about how to assemble and disassemble this puzzle.

INSTRUCTIONS:

Without breaking the bottle, unscrew the nut from the bolt and remove the dowel rod. No tools are necessary.

If you solve the puzzle, be prepared to put it back together when you finish.

FACILITATOR NOTES:
This is one of those problems that many people just think and stare at while one brave soul twists and turns the dowel rod in an attempt to use the bottle as a nut turning surface.

Consider offering this puzzle to a team. Give them time to plan a strategy before touching the bottle.

Avoid making the puzzle out of large bottles and large bolts. The weight of the bolt will crack or shatter your bottle.

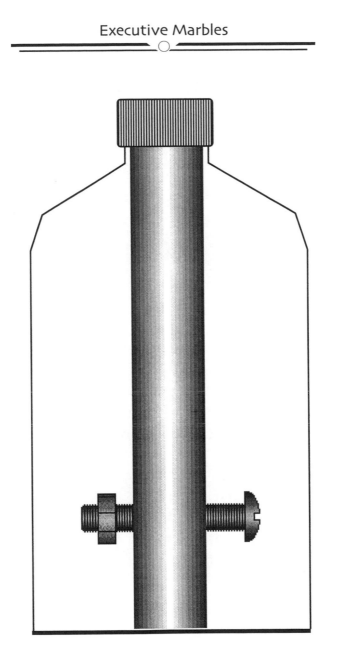

31

The Captain Is Coming

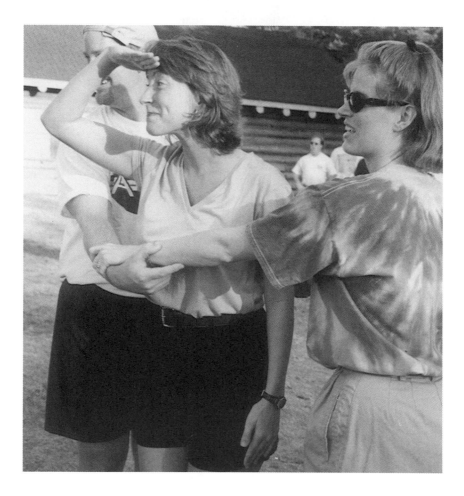

The Captain Is Coming

PROPS:
None

OBJECTIVE:
Break the ice or energize participants as they get into various groups.

HISTORY:
We first heard of this activity from an organization in California called Odyssey. Sometimes the dynamics of a game are so solid you know it is a winner. The Captain Is Coming is a winner.

INSTRUCTIONS:
The following is a great icebreaker and energizer for any group larger than 10. . . preferably larger than 20.

The facilitator plays the role of the captain and is the person who calls out the orders.

The following orders are several actions that the group does during the game depending on what the captain calls out:

"The captain is coming" - Everyone stands at attention and salutes the captain

"Swab the deck" - everyone acts like they are quickly mopping the floor

"Lighthouse" - Everyone gets into pairs. They stand facing each other, then turn in a circle while saying "boop, boop, boop"

"Man overboard" - Everyone gets into groups of three. Two people hold hands to form a circle around a third person who

stands looking for the man overboard.

"Row ashore" - Everyone gets into groups of four. They line up single file, facing the same direction and act as if they are rowing a boat together.

"Grub time" - Everyone gets into groups of five. They stand in a tight huddle and act as if they are spooning food into their mouths while quickly saying "grub, grub, grub".

For people who cannot get into a group during the game, they must **"walk the plank"**. These people walk over to a designated area and sing a pirate song. "Oheeeoh, a pirate's life for me" (repeat over and over)

The game is over when all but 2 have "walked the plank".

FACILITATOR NOTES:
For larger groups it is a good idea to have a "first mate" or two to help you direct people to walk the plank and keep singing the pirate song.

People "walk the plank" if there are too few or too many people in a group. For example, if there are six people in a "grub time" group, all six have to walk the plank.

Keep the action moving. Take just enough time for people walking the plank to be identified then call out another order.

Capture the Rope

Capture the Rope

PROPS:
- 2 Nylon webbings or strong rope 5+ feet (1.5 m) long
- 2 Figure-eight friction devices
- 2 Carabiners
- 1 Kernmantle climbing rope 60+ feet (18 m) long

OBJECTIVE:
1) Pull a rope completely out of two figure-eight friction devices. The team with the rope wins.
2) Teach about the effectiveness of these friction devices

PREPARATION:
Attach two figure-eights 5 feet apart to a large tree limb or horizontal pole approximately eight feet high. Thread the same rope through each of them. Put the end of the rope through the larger hole, around the waist and back through the larger hole of each figure-eight. (See illustration on page 39.)

Pull down the center section of the rope and even out the ends of the rope with the center section so that the left, right, and center sections are equal length.

INSTRUCTIONS:
Divide the group into three equal teams and send each team to each one of the rope sections.

Ask each team to stand at a section of rope and hold onto their section with at least one hand. No wrapping the rope around the hands, arms, necks, etc., is allowed.

RULZ:
Everyone must maintain contact with the rope except when moving to another

team.

If someone on another team tags you, you immediately join their team by letting go of the rope and joining onto their section.

A tag must be administered by hand, not foot.

The first team to pull the rope from both attachments wins. Go!!!!!

FACILITATOR NOTES:
As with most tag games the action is very quick to start but soon the strategies emerge.

Most of the time one of the three sections is absorbed by the other two sections and the three teams become two. After some back and forth tagging, usually one or two people remain at the end of the rope. They can usually outmaneuver the larger group, but the larger group has more hands to tag with.

One person can keep the rope from sliding through the figure-eight. It is amazing how well the "eights" work.

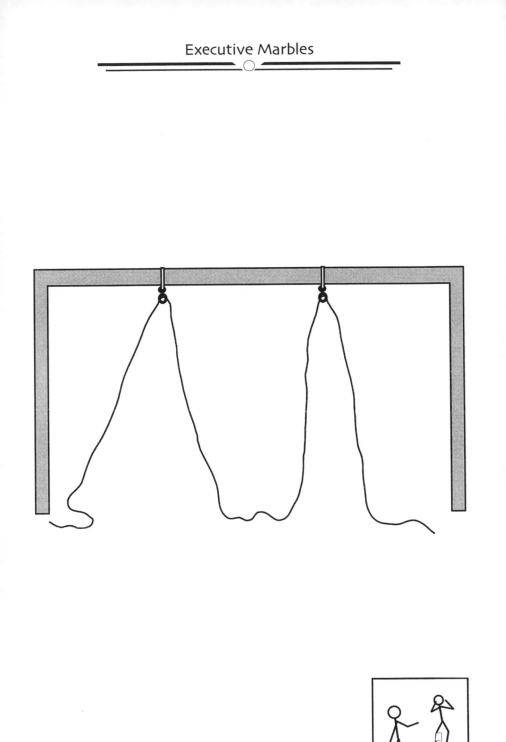

Afflictions/Consequences

Why?

Trainers often ask about the use of "handicaps" or "consequences" used during an experiential activity. Most of the time, they are looking for a greater variety of less-than-desirable results for participants to endure after making some mistake. Less often it is a question of ethics.

Why use afflictions as part of the training activities? Some of the strong benefits of experiential activities come from the speed and clarity of consequences. If "this" happens, then "that" is the result and I should learn to do "this" differently next time. For example: If you lose your balance on the beam and step on the ground, you lose your sight. Maybe you need to get better support from others next time.

Afflictions also make good use of metaphorical learning. I do not walk around the office with a blindfold over my eyes, but I do often become "blind" to situations because of my behavior.

Afflictions or consequences need to be a result of some action done by a team or an individual. Don't exasperate participants by pulling handicaps from the air to impose upon them without a clear reason. If a group is doing well, don't inflict some terrible something on them just because. Afflictions are tools that you should use wisely and with purpose.

Below is a list of several afflictions for those trainers who want to add to their tool kit.

The Senses
Blind - Participant puts on a bandanna so he cannot see
Partial blindness - Participant puts on a bandanna so he cannot see out of one eye. It causes the person to lose depth perception; however, they can see what is happening.
Tunnel Vision - Participant wears coke-bottle glasses or glasses with side-blinders
Mute - Participant cannot speak
Deaf - Participant cannot hear Place headphones and a small cassette player on a participant with the music turned up loudly

Verbal
Little Caesar's Disease or Double Talk - Participant says everything everything twice twice
Whiner - Participant says everything in a whiny voice
Contra Language - Everything the participant says is the opposite of what they mean.
Banana Language - After each word the person says the word "banana"
Weatherman's Speak - Everything the participant says is in the terminology of what a weather man might say during his forecast.
Opera - The participant can say anything as long as it is sung to a tune such as *Mary Had A Little Lamb*.
Jeopardy - Everything they say must be in the form of a question. (This one is great for directive participants.)

Time
Start Over - The group stops their progress and begins the activity again

<u>Loss Of Time</u> - For each mistake or "rework error" the group loses some portion of the time they have to finish the problem.

Body Usage

<u>Confusion</u> - Participant is instructed to walk backwards wherever he goes

<u>Unstoppable urge to hold the back of the neck</u> - Participant places a hand on the back of his neck and keeps it there

<u>Attachment Disorder</u> - One participant keeps hold of another participant during the activity

<u>Little Brother</u> - Everything one participant does or says is duplicated by another person

<u>Paralysis</u> - Participant stiffens a leg or arm and may not bend it

<u>Loss Of Limb</u> - The participant acts as if a part of his body is no longer there (arm, leg, hand, etc.).

Just for fun

<u>Loss Of All Body Hair</u>
<u>Sterility</u>
<u>Full Body Paralysis</u>

43

Champs Or Chumps

Champs Or Chumps

PROPS:
- A note card for each person
- A pen or pencil for each person

OBJECTIVE:
Fun way to get questions answered at the beginning of a retreat or training session.

HISTORY:
In my work with QuikTrip Corporation's manager development training we needed a way to give the managers all the introductory information they wanted and needed about the site and the training. We would start a ball toss while we all stood in a large circle. If you received the ball, it was your turn to ask a question that the staff would then answer. This process worked well at getting people the information, but we wanted a faster and more active process that became Champs Or Chumps.

INSTRUCTIONS:
Get into teams at tables.

Take a note card or two and write down a question you want answered about the facility, schedule, attendees, trainers, etc. Memorize the question and turn in the note card(s) to the trainer.

The trainer explains that everyone has 10 minutes to get their questions answered and to find out the answers to everyone else's questions. Any resource is all right to use.

At the end of the time, a trainer will randomly select 4 questions from the pool of all the questions possible to ask each table team. The team will need to answer

the questions correctly.

Go to each group and hopefully they will answer most of the questions.

The trainer has the option of tossing repeat questions.

If no one knows an answer, give the group the answers after the game.

FACILITATOR NOTES:
In most cases there will be several duplicate questions.

Have a list of normal questions and answers in mind to give to the whole group after the activity in case no one asked some of the more important questions.

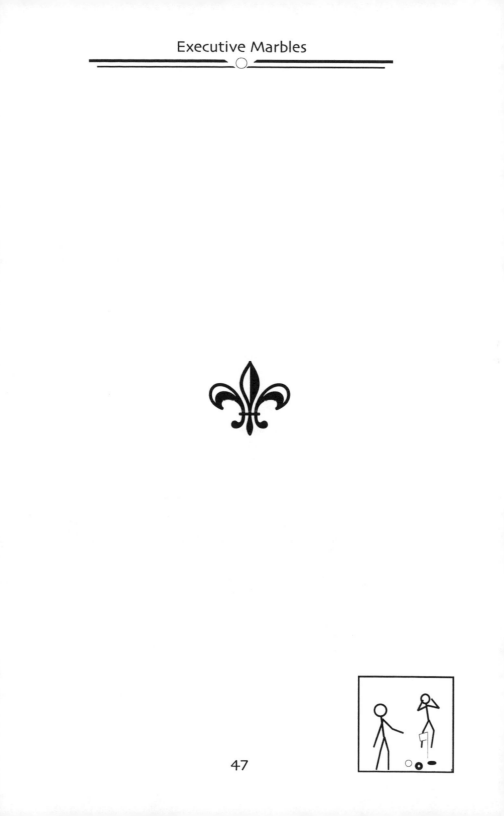

Command Performance

Command Performance

PROPS:
You will need copies of the activity template at the end of these instructions and a pen or pencil for each participant.

OBJECTIVE:
Meet everyone in the room.

PREPARATION:
Number name tags for all the participants. As people enter the room, pass out the tags. Another option is to ask people to number off and number their own paper or name tag.

INSTRUCTIONS:
Everyone needs to have a different number starting with number 1 and going up to the number of people in the group.

Take a pen or pencil and write your number on the first line of your Command Performance sheet. Now, number the rest of the blanks from your number up to the highest number and then start back at 1. For example, if there were 25 people in the group and I was number 23, I would start with 23 then write 24 and 25, then 1, 2, 3, 4, and so on.

Now that you have the numbers on your page, find the people with those numbers and follow the instructions on the sheet. You may start anywhere on the page and try to get through all the items in approximately 5 minutes.

FACILITATOR NOTES:
This activity gets everyone into action at the same time. Do not worry about what each person is doing in the group.

The things the Command Performance sheet asks each person to do can be a challenge for some people. Most of the time people will enjoy doing things that seem a little silly as long as they do not feel watched or forced.

Command Performance

Place your name and number here _____

Introduce yourself to _____

Shake hands with _____

Give _____ a back rub.

Compliment _____ on their shoes.

Describe the ways that _____ reminds you of Albert Einstein.

Get _____ to laugh.

Introduce _____ to someone else in the room.

Compare arm spans with _____

Tell _____ what animal you admire the most.

Do a quick magic trick for _____

Lie to _____

Point your finger at _____

Maintain a straight face in front of _____ for 3 seconds.

Do a "high-five" with _____

Sing a song to _____

Wink at _____

Sneak up behind _____

Stick your tongue at _____

A Fun Scenario

The following scenario is meant to liven up any crossover event. A crossover event is one where half of a group starts at one end of a here-to-there activity and the other half starts at the other end. The two groups pass each other. You can also string two here-to-there activities together. A group starts on each end and crosses both events from opposite directions.

PROPS:
- 1 Tummy scratcher -- a stick or hairbrush or be creative
- 1 Supple ceremonial ring -- a loop of rope or inner tube or again be creative
- A slip of paper with the rest of the scenario on it for each team

FACILITATOR NOTES:
Read the first part of the scenario to the entire group. Make sure they understand the rules of the crossover event(s). Then give each group one of the slips of paper and the props for "the rest of the story".

People usually look suspiciously at the other half of the group. You have placed them in an inconsistent situation. On the one hand there is the message about working as a team and the strong reference to customers and suppliers. On the other hand the tribes are supposed to be dangerous and the other group has been handed secret information. Now you expect the groups to cross a space covered with molten lava while trying not to be "recognized" for who they really are. This is starting to sound like a soap opera!

People will project their own beliefs and values onto

other people when they do not have all the information. This scenario leaves many gaps in the information about the other group. All of this guessing and projection turns into rich discussion material after the activity. How did they cooperate or compete? How was information shared or concealed? What were some obstacles to increased trust? What did people focus on? How are these situations like the workplace?

⚡

The Land of Er

Two tribes live in the land of Er -- the Supply and the Cussing Tummies. The Supply tribe and the Cussing Tummies have co-existed in this land for centuries. As they do every year on this day, the two peoples are joining in a high ceremony to exchange gifts and enter into each other's territory for the remainder of the year.

Every year the Supply Ers share a ceremonial tummy scratcher with their partner tribe and receive a supple ceremonial ring from the Cussing Tummies.

As each person enters the new land, he is expected to greet the other tribe's members with the ceremonial hand shake.

Supply Ers are named for their inability to throw anything away, because, "You never know when you might need it."

Cussing Tummy Ers (Cuss Tum Ers) are named for their colorful language and extreme laughter.

Both tribes are very fierce and dangerous to any other cultures.

Both tribes are also highly accomplished

53

team players. They can spot non-teamness in an instant. To maintain their team skills they always exchange territories at a location where they can demonstrate team problem solving. Sometimes a few people are disfigured in the process, but the tribe learns from their actions.

The customary exchange spot is the one you see before you. Notice the molten lava between where you are now and your destination. AVOID THIS POISONOUS LAVA or terrible consequences may occur.

Cuss Tum Ers
You have found yourselves in the land of the Cussing Tummies. Although you are not really from this area, your identity is still unknown to the natives. Your task is to reach safety by traversing into the land of the Supply. Fortunately, the Supply tribe currently thinks you are Cussing Tummies.

Remember to be on your best team behavior or the Supply tribe will recognize you as being from another land. Oh, and you better think about that ceremonial hand shake before you reach the middle of the crossing.

Good luck!!!!

+-+

Supply Ers
You have found yourselves in the land of the Supply tribe. Although you are not really from this area, your identity is still unknown to the natives. Your task is to reach safety by traversing into the the land of the Cussing Tummies. Fortunately, the Cussing Tummy tribe currently thinks you are Supply Ers.

Remember to be on your best team behavior or the Cussing Tummies will recognize you as being from another land. Oh, and you better think about that ceremonial hand shake before you reach the middle of the crossing.

Good luck!!!!

Communalities

Communalities

PROPS:
None

OBJECTIVE:
The group finds out what they have in common, from general to specific information.

HISTORY:
We often work with people from varied backgrounds. A community support organization asked me to focus their volunteers on the things they had in common. In reality we are all connected in some direct or indirect way, so this simple activity was born to make the point that whether you are talking in terms of systems thinking or communities, we have many things in common even if it is difficult to understand what until we get involved.

INSTRUCTIONS:
We are going to do a quick activity to see what we have in common as a group. We will start together as one group then I will ask you to divide into two groups and have each smaller group come up with something they all have in common that also relates to the previous topic. When we have completed a few rounds, we will be in groups of 2 or 3 people and I will ask each small group to share what they have in common.

Decide upon one thing you all have in common. Check to make sure everyone actually has that one thing in common.

Divide in half (two groups) and ask each half to come up with something you have in common that is within the first category.

Divide each of those groups in half and ask each group to come up with something they have in common that relates to the last category.

Continue this process until you have groups of twos or threes.

When the groups are as small as they can get, ask each group to announce their last commonality. Expect a wide range of responses that may seem to have no connection to the group's original response.

FACILITATOR NOTES:

I tend to move from group to group as they make their decisions. I often ask for groups to raise their hands when they are ready for the next round. Even in a group of 30 people you will end up with 14 small groups at the end and it can be a challenge to manage.

The number of times the groups will divide is really not many. A group of 30 people will only go through 4 rounds before they finally split into groups of pairs and triads. A group of 200 would only need 7 rounds and a group of 1 million would only take 19 rounds. . . but you better bring your lunch.

Creative Mind Benders

Creative Mind Benders

PROPS:
- A sheet of blank paper
- A pen or pencil for each person

OBJECTIVE:
Encourage creative thinking to solve a simple problem.

HISTORY:
The following puzzles have been around for many years and I have seen them show up in a variety of seminars and trainings. The interesting thing I have noticed is how people will create their own solutions if they are not told the "answer" too quickly. I think we often stop at one solution instead of looking for alternatives when we can. Several of the solutions came from participants after I told them there were several solutions to each problem.

INSTRUCTIONS:

Problem #1 - Move any one of the bars below to make both sides of this equation equal. The equal sign is not a bar and cannot be moved. You may consider the "V" one or two bars.

$$I = V I I$$

Problem #2 - Add one line to the IX below to turn it into a 6.

FACILITATOR NOTES:

Above are two puzzles that I have used when training creativity. I especially like them because they both have more than one acceptable answer. For each puzzle I have provided some of the solutions people in my workshops have proposed. Some of the "answers" are straight forward and obvious; others require an extra open mind. Nevertheless, I will list the answers and give the participant's rationale for why the answers are correct. See how many you can come up with. The solutions start on page 205.

The Creativity Paradigm:

From one perspective, creativity is the ability to see something another person sees in a different way. For the creative person, common things and issues are given new meaning. It's not that the creative person necessarily invents or constructs something as much as they see it with new insight.

Comedians use this strategy in their observations of everyday life. Some of my favorite comical questions from Gallagher include the following: "Why do they call them apartments when they're so close together?" "Why do they call it a shipment when it's carried in a truck and 'cargo' when it's carried on a boat?" In these examples, he has taken our normal definition of words and shifted the meaning (or at least our perspective of the meaning). Jerry Seinfeld has made a very successful career out of seeing daily situations in a new way.

Much of what I'm talking about is changing paradigms. A paradigm is a model, pattern, or set of ideas that describes some aspect of the world. Changing your own definition of something or seeing things in a new way is often called a "paradigm shift". The shift can happen on many dimensions from finding a new use for a hammer to changing the rules of mathematics to solve a problem. These "shifts" give many companies a competitive advantage both in internal operations and new products and services.

Cubicles

Cubicles

PROPS:
For each group of 10 to 20 people you need
- 24 midaronis (12 full length foam pool noodles cut in half)
- A stopwatch.

OBJECTIVE:
Build a cube as quickly as possible using foam noodles.

HISTORY:
Cubicles is a variation of a blindfold exercise from *50 Ways To Use Your Noodle* called 3-D Noodle Shapes. We needed a fast activity to illustrate the wisdom for teams to establish clear roles and responsibilities. It was amazing how quickly teams could build a cube from 24 foam noodles.

INSTRUCTIONS:
Split the group in half and give 12 midaronis to each group.

Rulz:
No one may touch the noodles before the start of each round. When you hear "Go!" build a cube out of your group's noodles as quickly as possible. Shout when you finish. Go!!

The two groups quickly construct their noodle shapes (hopefully without butting heads).

Try a couple or three rounds and see how quickly the groups can make the cubes.

Now, combine both groups and their resources and ask them to build a bigger cube using their 24 noodles. After a

couple or three rounds, compare the times to the smaller cube times.

Often the larger cube takes less time to construct than the smaller ones.

FACILITATOR NOTES:

In general, a team should be able to make one of the small cubes in 2 seconds and two teams with their combined resources can build one large cube in under 2 seconds.

As with any energizing activity, it is helpful for the facilitator to keep things moving and be an energetic model for the teams.

I often move through the small cube building rounds fairly quickly and then give a little time for the combined groups to organize themselves before starting the bigger cube building.

This is a good activity to use with two departments that are merging or companies that are merging.

VARIATIONS:

If you have enough people and noodles for three cubes, you can try to get one giant cube made at the end. The 36 noodle cube will be almost 8 feet tall.

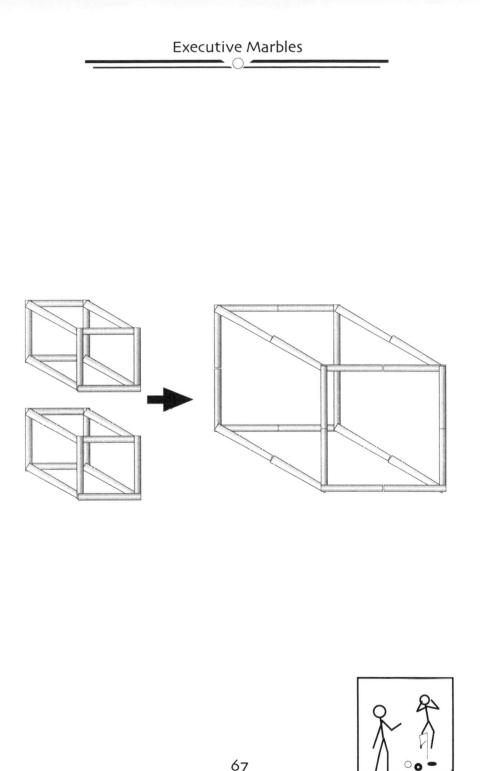

Executive Marbles

Executive Marbles

PROPS:
Outdoor version
- Billiard balls, one per person
- 5 Marker flags
- Marker for the starting shots (a tee off)

Indoor version
- Tennis balls with 12 pennies inside each, one per person
  (Carefully cut a small slit in a tennis ball and push 12 pennies into it. The pennies will add weight to the ball and slow its rolling ability. They're great for juggling too!)
- 5 Paper squares or circles approximately 4 inches in diameter.
- Masking tape

OBJECTIVE:
Toss a ball into five consecutive holes and back again while knocking opponent's balls out of the way and avoid being hit yourself.

HISTORY:
This game originates from a Native American game called Cherokee Marbles. The Cherokee Indians make their own game balls out of stone. Each year the tribe gathers at a festival in Tahlequah, Oklahoma where they play many games including "Marbles". I understand that at the 1996 festival some of the elders played the game four-and-a-half hours before someone won. The version described below is a simplified variation of the original game.

PREPARATION:
Outdoor version
You are going to make a five-hole marble course that forms an "L" shape. There

needs to be approximately 40 feet between each hole. Take one of the billiard balls and place it on the ground where you want the first hole. Step on the ball so that it forms a depression in the ground approximately an inch deep. You may have to dig away some of the hard dirt or grass roots. Place a flag six inches from the hole. Forty feet is close to sixteen normal steps. Step off to the next location, make another hole and so on. Put a marker (something like a flag or hula hoop) on the ground twenty feet from the first hole to designate where the game begins.

Indoor version
Construct a course similar to the one described above. Most people do not like you to put holes in their floor, so just secure a square or circle of paper to the floor with tape or just make a square on the floor with tape. A weighted tennis ball will have to stay on the paper or within the tape and not roll out to count as a completed shot. Use masking tape to mark the number of each goal if you want. The "L" shape and the distances between holes are flexible. Do what you need to with the space you have.

INSTRUCTIONS:
The goal is to get your ball into holes one through five and then return to hole four through the gauntlet of other players in reverse order until you finally make a winning shot back at hole number one.

Each person starts at the starting marker by tossing his ball toward the first hole. Taking turns, everyone shoots. If someone's ball hits another ball on the first bounce or before the first bounce, he gets another shot before the next person has a turn. There are no limits on how many times your ball may hit other balls.

Make sure people know you are tossing your ball. Let's not make helmets a requirement.

A shot- Your feet are together on the spot where your ball previously landed. Nothing else is supporting your body. Underhand or overhand throws are fine. You must let go of the ball. If your ball doesn't go into a hole or hit another ball, it stays on the ground where it stops.

Another shot - Your ball hits someone else's ball on the first bounce or before, so you can take another shot. Most of the time you will hit someone's ball before your ball hits the ground. In taller grass or leafy areas, many teams establish a "click rule". The click rule states that someone must hear your ball click against another ball before you can claim to get another shot. In tall grass or leaf covered areas a person's ball may move because it was pushed by the grass instead of hit by a ball.

A completed shot - Your ball goes in the hole it is supposed to. If you can reach the hole, you may place the ball in the hole instead of tossing it. Pick up your ball and wait for your next turn to shoot. You can only complete a shot with your own ball. If someone hits someone else's ball into a hole, remove the ball from the hole and place it near the flag.

As an **option**, you may "slam dunk" your ball into the hole. A slam dunk is when a person falls to complete a shot. The ball must touch the ground before the person does and he must let go of the ball. It can be painful, but it does give you another 2 feet of distance if you are willing to smite the earth.

A winning shot - You have completed the shots for holes 1-2-3-4-5-4-3-2 in sequence and now you make the last completed shot at hole 1. Congratulations!

TEAM STYLE INSTRUCTIONS:

Playing executive marbles in teams is fun and full of complex strategy. A team of 2-4 people plays against another team of equal size. With billiard balls, you can play with stripes against solids.

In this game, a team wins when any one of the team's balls makes it to holes number 1-2-3-4-5-4-3-2 and back to hole one.

Each person shoots <u>with his own ball</u> and everyone takes turns so that the teams alternate (1st person stripes, 1st person solids, 2nd person stripes, 2nd person solids, etc.)

The shooting rules are the same as the individual game written above. The team decides the strategies. Do we all try to complete every hole? Does only one of us complete every hole while the others play as defenders or offenders?

The more you play, the more strategies you realize to win.

FACILITATOR NOTES:

It is a good idea to wander around answering questions as people start to play. I have discovered that people really get competitive while they play this game, so feel free to copy the rules of play and have them available for everyone. It is better for everyone, especially the facilitator, that the participants know the rules at the beginning.

Observe the group dynamics throughout the activity and make a few notes. Alliances change, agreements emerge. It is interesting how many people hit other people's marbles as hard as possible every time when a series of controlled taps is often the wiser strategy.

I like to use this activity with people who are usually independent from the rest of the groups, but really need to see how they can work together to "win".

VARIATIONS:
This activity usually takes about an hour to play in the teams. You can decrease the time necessary by placing only four flags instead of five. In general, the closer the holes are to each other, the longer the activity will last.

When playing the team version, I usually have one team play against another. You can have three teams of three play on the same course. It will take a little longer, but it keeps more people together on the same course.

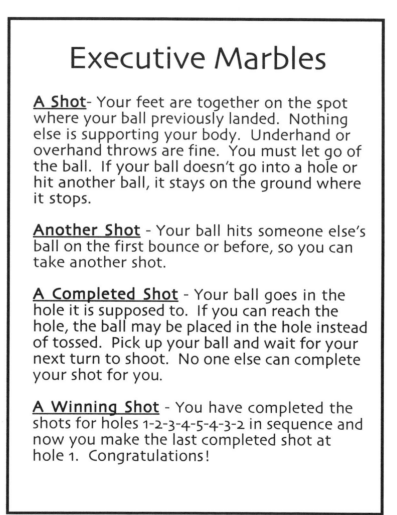

Executive Marbles

A Shot- Your feet are together on the spot where your ball previously landed. Nothing else is supporting your body. Underhand or overhand throws are fine. You must let go of the ball. If your ball doesn't go into a hole or hit another ball, it stays on the ground where it stops.

Another Shot - Your ball hits someone else's ball on the first bounce or before, so you can take another shot.

A Completed Shot - Your ball goes in the hole it is supposed to. If you can reach the hole, the ball may be placed in the hole instead of tossed. Pick up your ball and wait for your next turn to shoot. No one else can complete your shot for you.

A Winning Shot - You have completed the shots for holes 1-2-3-4-5-4-3-2 in sequence and now you make the last completed shot at hole 1. Congratulations!

Dynamic Flying Squirrel

Dynamic Flying Squirrel

Warning: Do not use this activity unless you have a clear working knowledge of the equipment used for the activity (i.e., tying knots, belaying, attaching carabiners to safety anchors, using rope pulleys, harnessing). The activity may be perceived as risky. However, if it is properly prepared and operated the actual safety risk is minimal.

PROPS:
- 1 rope pulley
- 9 carabiners
- A minimum of 5 webbing loops or lanyards
- A minimum of 6 seat harnesses
- 1 chest harness
- 1 static rope (height of safety cable X 2 + 15 feet)
- 1 helmet for the flyer
- 1 marker

OBJECTIVE:
A team lifts team members, one at a time, to a height of 35+ feet within two seconds.

HISTORY:
I had read about the Flying Squirrel in Karl Rohnke's *Bottomless Bag* book. Facilitators used the event as a method to lift people who could not climb. It gave anyone the experience of heights. A few years ago I talked to John English of Project Adventure about the event. He told me about a group using it much as it is described below. They set-up the event next to a lake. The "squirrel" would run and jump as if he were going to land in the water. Just before he would have landed, the belay swept him up and out over the water. I couldn't wait to try it. This activity is quite a rush.

PREPARATION:
Locate 2 support poles (trees) at least 20 feet apart with a safety cable strung between them as high as safely possible. Attach a free-wheel rope pulley to the safety cable and run a static rope through the pulley. The rope should be long enough to touch the ground with both ends plus approximately 15 feet. Slide the pulley halfway between the support poles (trees).

Tie a bowline on a bight or figure eight on a bight at both ends of the rope. On the flyer's end put 2-3 carabiners. On the lifters' end, put at least 5 webbing loops of varied length and a carabiner on each loop.

Hook a weight on the flyer's end and, holding the webbing end, hoist it to within 5 feet of the pulley. Mark the ground with a distinctly visible marker of some sort. Lower the weight back down to the ground and detach the weight. This measurement determines how far the lifting team will travel before stopping. You can slowly lift a person in the group to get the distance measurement if you wish.

INSTRUCTIONS:
Hook the rope to the back of the flyer's seat and chest harness. Hook a webbing loop to the back of each lifter's seat harness.

The lift crew should stand near the flyer facing the marker where they will be running. The flyer should be facing the lifters.

Basically, the lifters will run toward the marker while the flyer runs past the lifters. When the slack is removed from the rope (ideally, when the flyer is directly underneath the pulley), the flyer will be sucked into the air and swing back and forth. Lifters will <u>stop</u> when they get to the marker. The marker keeps the lifters from running too far and sucking the flyer through the pulley (Not really, but it wouldn't feel good if they ran too far.).

Make sure that the rope will not be crossed at the time of lift-off.

When the experience is over, the lifters slowly walk back to the start to lower the flyer.

FACILITATOR NOTES:
Be aware of the following three safety issues:

1) Flyers could swing into a support pole if the direction of their swing changes. Once the flyer is at maximum height, their swinging will stop after a few seconds.

2) Someone in a group of lifters could fall between the starting point and the marker. Make sure you choose level ground and inform your lifters of the possibility of falling.

3) Spotters standing near the support poles can help stop a swinging flyer from contacting a pole. The side to side swinging rarely occurs, but this precaution is good to use until you have determined the dynamics of your particular location.

The equipment list calls for static rope. You can use dynamic rope, but you do not have quite as much control over the timing of the lift. The dynamic rope stretches more before it lifts.

SCENARIO:
Superman or Superwoman try outs? Let's just make sure it is not George Of The Jungle try outs.

VARIATIONS:
Rather than the flyer just running before being lifted, set a soft cone or ball on the ground. Have them try to run and grab

the object before being lifted. This variation gives the lifters some incentive to move quickly so the flyer cannot quite grab the object.

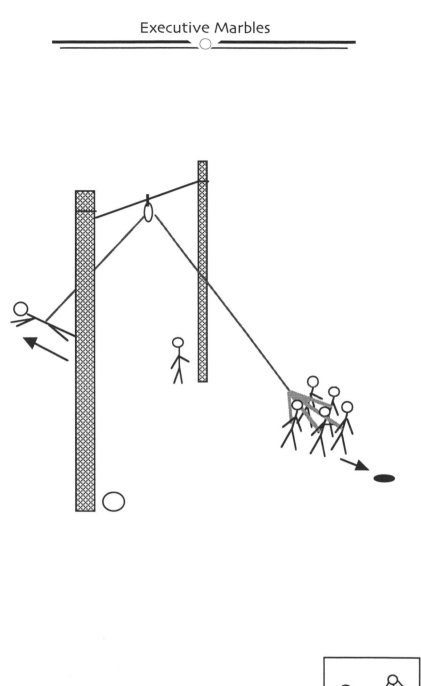

81

Survival Of The Fittest

Sometimes an e-mail gets sent that really makes you wonder.

Date: 09/19 7:20 AM
Received: 09/19 7:26 AM
From: John Woodland, ClarkPines@aol.com

Got this from a friend at BCM this morning.

I just received this from a friend at Bucknell U. and had to pass it on because it kind of applies.....

Whenever I get a package of plain M&Ms, I make it my duty to continue the strength and robustness of the candy as a species. To this end, I hold M&M duels. Taking two candies between my thumb and forefinger, I apply pressure, squeezing them together until one of them cracks and splinters. That is the "loser," and I eat the inferior one immediately. The winner gets to go another round.

I have found that, in general, the brown and red M&Ms are tougher, and the newer blue ones are genetically inferior. I have hypothesized that the blue M&Ms as a race cannot survive long in the intense theater of competition that is the modern candy and snack-food world. Occasionally I will get a mutation, a candy that is misshapen, or pointier, or flatter than the rest. Almost invariably this proves to be a weakness, but on very rare occasions it gives the candy extra strength. In this way, the species continues to adapt to its environment. When I reach the end of the pack, I am left with one M&M, the strongest of the herd. Since it would make no sense to eat this one as well, I pack it neatly in an envelope and send it to M&M Mars, A Division of Mars, Inc., Hackettstown, NJ 17840-1503 USA, along with a 3x5 card reading, "Please use this M&M for breeding purposes."

This week they wrote back to thank me, and sent me a coupon for a free 1/2 pound bag of plain M&Ms. I consider this "grant money." I have set aside the weekend for a grand tournament. From a field of hundreds, we will discover the True Champion. There can be only one.

Hot Air Balloons

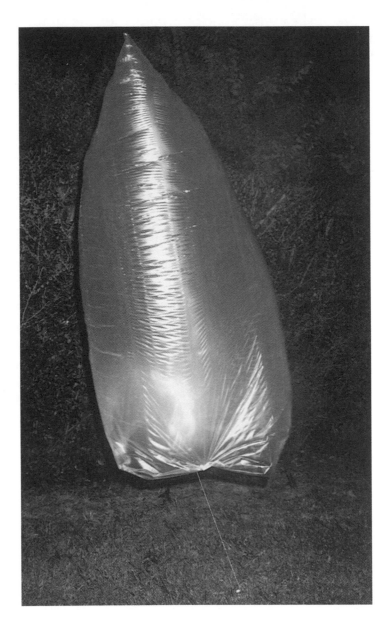

Hot Air Balloons

PROPS:
Each group needs:
- A 32 to 55 gallon (121 to 208 liter) plastic trash bag (most building supply stores have clear bags)
- Metal clothes hanger
- 3 sheets of paper or fuel container as described below
- Masking tape
- 3 feet (.91 m) of string or fishing line
- A 2 foot (.61 m) wire fishing leader or other flexible wire
- A weight more than 5 ounces (142 g) (like fishing sinkers)
- 1 ounce (29.6 ml) of camp stove fuel
- A cigarette lighter
- Miscellaneous stuff like thread, bubble gum, marbles, skewer sticks, etc.

OBJECTIVE:
Build a hot air balloon from the materials provided, launch it, and keep it in the air.

HISTORY:
I first heard of this activity using birthday candles, skewer sticks, and a dry cleaner's bag. I had to try it, but I had a hard time keeping the bag in the air and wax off my carpet. After several experiments in my garage I found a good balance of fire power and materials. At a conference in Louisiana we launched several balloons from an open field in a state park. The wind was still. . . at least up to an altitude of 100 feet. One of the balloons caught an air current and began floating over the forest. Several people ran through the woods and retrieved it several hundred feet away. Fortunately the trees were wet and the fuel gone. Now I attach the balloons to a

85

wire to avoid any more rescue missions.

PREPARATION:
Find a nonflammable location to launch the balloons. Fill a bucket with water and immerse towels into it. Have one towel per group. The wet towels can smother a flame quickly if needed.
Gather the materials and place them where the teams will be working.
Indoors, check for smoke detectors or sprinkler systems. I don't think you want to set off a sprinkler system in some hotel training room. The paper will smoke, but the fuel container described at the end of these instructions will not smoke nearly as much and it is reusable.

Things to consider:
Don't launch the balloons when there is any wind. The balloons will fly erratically and might catch something on fire.

Assess the maturity of the participants and the supervision required in a worst case scenario.

Quickly educate the group on the critical issues for a successful flight. Some of the issues include the following:
- The larger the hot air container (the bag) the more weight the balloon will lift.
- Plastic burns, paper burns, string burns, so prevent a towering inferno.
- The lighter the balloon, the easier it is to get off the ground.
- It works better to heat the air inside the balloon than to heat the air outside.
- Stop, drop, and roll.

INSTRUCTIONS:
Give the teams of 2 to 5 participants the building materials. Ask them to take up to 15 minutes to

design and build a hot air balloon with the materials provided. The balloon should float no higher than 5 feet (1.5 m) off the floor. No team should ignite its fuel until everyone is ready.

The fuel may be in the form of paper with some flammable fluid on it wrapped at the bottom of the bag <u>or</u> the reusable fuel container described at the end of this activity. Wait to put fluid into the containers until you are ready to launch.

After the 15 minutes, instruct the teams to light the fuel simultaneously. Watch for the first balloon to keep itself aloft. Watch for which team's balloon stays up the longest. Finally, watch for any balloons that might catch fire. You will need to cover them with a wet towel.

Achievements Recognized
• In the air the longest
• In the air the quickest
• In the air
• The Hindenburg

FACILITATOR NOTES:
I have used this activity many times with teams. It is an activity few people would ever try on their own. It needs to be a very controlled situation and it certainly sparks excitement as people light their fuel and watch the balloon fill with hot air.

The large plastic bags take a minute to lift off. Once they are aloft, they usually hover about a minute. Balloons often melt before the fuel completely burns out.

VARIATIONS:
For some high adventure use a fishing rod and reel with your balloon. Go outside on a still night (or day) and attach a wire

leader to the fuel container and attach your rod and reel line to the wire leader. Light the balloon and let out the line to allow the balloon to float as high as possible. If it starts to go where you don't want it, just reel the balloon back to you. You can often launch the same balloon several times. You can expect the balloon to ascend to 200 feet or more.

Making an indoor fuel container

You need:
- 1 aluminum soda can
- Scissors
- Pliers
- Wire as thin or thinner than a coat hanger
- Stainless steel or brass wool like used for cleaning dishes (coarse, not fine)

Carefully cut around the can 1 inch (2.54 cm) from the bottom. The bottom of the can will be the fuel reservoir. Make at least 8 cuts 1/2 inch (1.27 cm) down toward the bottom of the can (See diagram below.)

Make a wire ring the same diameter as the can plus enough wire to make four small loops that the participants will later use to attach this fuel container to their balloon.

Twist the wire so that it has four small loops. Place the wire ring around the base of the can. Bend every-other flap of aluminum out and down so that they hold the wire ring in place.

Tear or cut off just enough wire wool to cover the inside of the fuel container. Bend the other aluminum flaps in to hold the wool in place. The wool keeps the fuel from splashing over the sides and helps distribute the flame.

Tie a 3 foot piece of flexible wire around the container

vertically and secure it on the bottom side. Leave a tail of wire hanging under the container. At the end of the tail attach a weight. This weight will keep the balloons from rising more than the length of the tail.

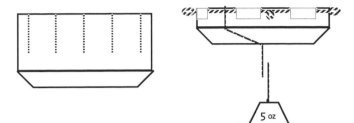

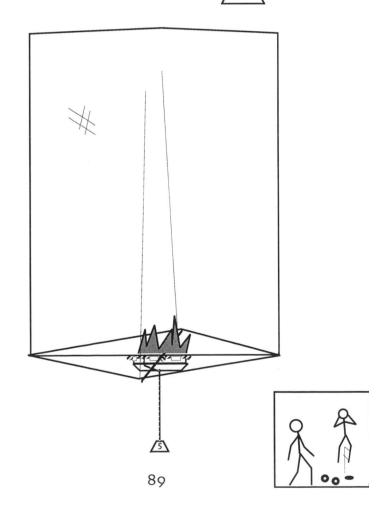

Identity Crisis

Identity Crisis

PROPS:
- Masking tape
- Markers to write names on the tape
- One object for each person (tennis balls work well)
- Rope for a starting line
- A bandana for each person
- One hula hoop

OBJECTIVE:
Guide someone into an area to blindly retrieve your ball or theirs.

HISTORY:
Kip Prichard introduced this activity at a state games conference in 1994. We all had a great time playing it. My partner and I decided to place our tennis balls on the far left side of the hoop so that they would be easy for us to find. It would have worked, too, if it hadn't been for all those other tennis balls rolling around in the hoop. I had a hard enough time locating the hoop much less my partner's ball!

PREPARATION:
Select a site where there is open space between the partners and their objectives (hoop and balls). Place a hula hoop or a type of large container approximately 25 feet from a starting line. Provide each person in the group with one tennis ball, a strip of masking tape, and a pen or marker.

INSTRUCTIONS:
Divide into pairs.

Take a piece of tape and stick it to your tennis ball, then write your name on the tape.

Place your ball in the hoop and come back to the starting line.

This is a race. Each person is to retrieve the object with their partner's name on it or their own name. One partner has the resources of sight and speech, but cannot cross the line during the activity unless he is blindfolded; the other can move to the hoop but is blindfolded.

Each blind player must safely go to the object pile (no running please), pick an object and display it to his partner to see if it belongs to either the sighted or blind partner. If it does belong to one of them, the blind partner returns to the line with the ball and the partners exchange roles. If not, he continues to search for the item until he retrieves it.

Balls must be carried, not thrown, and only one ball at a time may be transported.

FACILITATOR NOTES:
In most cases some balls get bumped or kicked out of the hula-hoop. Quickly return the misplaced balls to the hula-hoop.

With a little careful wording you can change this partner activity into a whole team activity. In the team version, a blind person can get a ball and be guided to its sighted owner. The challenge then becomes how quickly can all the balls be recovered. Groups as large as 30 people can usually complete the task is 35 seconds or less.

Make sure you are in a place where you can be really noisy.

Issues:
Frustration tolerance, noise, trust, teamwork, communication, problem solving

VARIATIONS:

Instead of a starting line, use a large circle of rope approximately 80 feet long to go around the hula-hoop in the center of the circle. Anyone inside the rope must be blind. This variation requires more space, but keeps groups of up to 30 participants focused since they can see each other around the circle.

Insanity

Insanity

PROPS:
- 5 hula hoops - one in the middle, the others at the compass points from the center hoop.
- Assorted playful items - approximately 2 or 3 times the number of participants.

OBJECTIVE:
Get all the items from the center hoop into your own hoop.

PREPARATION:
Arrange the hoops with several feet between them (the greater number of participants, the more space between the hula hoops).

INSTRUCTIONS:
Divide the participants into four groups. Have each group go to one of the outside hoops. Place all the items into the center hoop. Give the participants the following instructions:

1) The object is to get all the items you see in the center hoop into your own hoop.
2) Each person may carry only one item at a time.
3) You may not throw items.
4) Once the center hoop is empty, you may take items from any other hoops.
5) You may <u>not</u> guard any of the hoops. If you are on the bottom of a pile of people, you're doing it wrong.
6) You win when <u>all</u> the items are in your hoop.

Then, without giving the participants any time to strategize, yell "Go!" Allow the resulting frenzy to go on about 1 - 2 minutes, then stop the activity. Tell the group that you will give them 2 minutes

to strategize, then you will start round 2.

At the end of the 2 minutes, start the next round. If more rounds are necessary for the participants to make the shift from competition to cooperation, continue the sequence of 1 - 2 minutes of activity and 2 minutes of strategizing.

FACILITATOR NOTES:

Most groups "win" by everyone placing their hoops on top of each other and putting all the objects in them. Everyone wins!

There are other ways a group can "win". One group can intimidate the others or out last them. I have seen an alliance form between two groups who won working together against the other two groups, although this scenario is very rare.

Various issues may be the focus of your debrief. The specific goals of the group may determine the direction of your discussion, or the dynamics present during the activity may suggest the direction. Nevertheless, here are a few issues that typically surface from this experience:

1) Futility of the work - impossible task
2) Competition vs. cooperation - shifting
     paradigms
3) Who is the "team"
4) Sabotage (someone holds back an item so no
     one wins)
5) Communication processes
6) Trust

Certainly, this is not a comprehensive list of topics, only the more common ones. So, as always, when facilitating these activities, be prepared for anything!

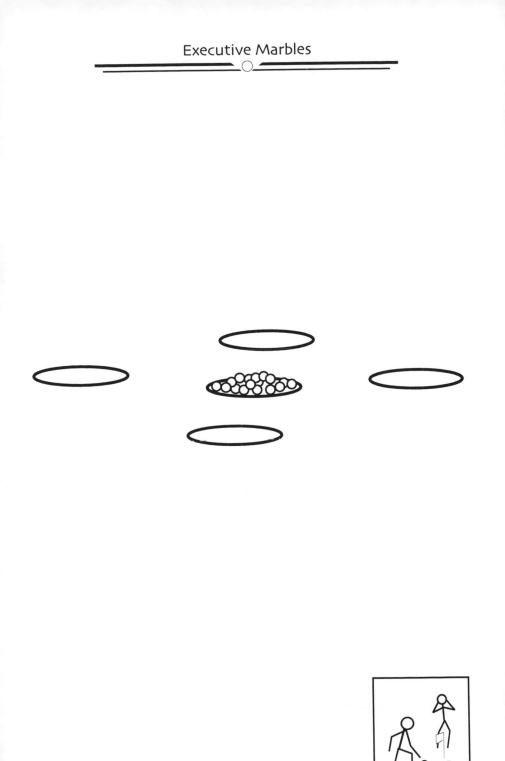

Juggling Steps

Juggling Steps

PROPS:
• Up to 3 balls for each person
It is a good idea to use balls that do not bounce well such as bean bags, Koosh balls, or tennis balls with 12 or more pennies inserted into them. Tennis clubs are a great source of cheap tennis balls. They will usually give them away when they go flat.

OBJECTIVE:
Learn the process for juggling. Key learning objectives tend to be: establishing structure within perceived chaos, focus, teamwork, cooperation, communication, consistency, time and resource management.

HISTORY:
I attended an International Conference for the Association for Experiential Education in Austin, Texas where I learned many of the juggling steps. The guy who led the workshop was expecting about 20 people and ended up having almost 80 people attend. I was impressed how well he handled the group by himself as he got everyone involved in the learning process. I left the workshop knowing how to juggle, but not yet being able to juggle. After several hours of practice, I finally became a juggling maniac. I juggled bean bags. I pushed pennies into tennis balls (see Executive Marbles). I filled tennis balls with lead shot to add weight to my exercise. I scared my wife, my dog, and my co-workers, but it sure has been a fun skill to know.

INSTRUCTIONS:
The following process does not describe much technique. There are numerous books on the market for the serious juggler. This is a speedy process for

several people at once to learn juggling with balls.

Everyone stands in circle
The facilitator will need to tell the participants when to toss their ball. A "1, 2, 3, toss," works well.

Everyone takes a ball in his right hand and tosses it to the left hand of the person on his left. Repeat 3 or four times - stopping after each toss. Encourage head-high tosses.

Everyone takes a ball in his left hand and tosses it to the right hand of the person on his right. Repeat 3 or four times - stopping after each toss.

Everyone takes a ball in his right hand and tosses it to the left hand of the person to his left but this time skip the person to your immediate left. Repeat 3 or four times - stopping after each toss.

Switch directions and hands. Repeat 3 or four times - stopping after each toss.

Stand side by side with a partner.
Take one ball and toss it to the "imaginary corner" of your partner. (See diagram.) Take turns tossing it back and forth. Don't use your inside hands.

Take two balls. Decide who will toss first. When the first ball hits the "imaginary corner" your partner should toss his ball. Establish a pattern of toss-toss-pause, toss-toss-pause, toss-toss-pause.

Stand on the other side of your partner and practice with the other hand.

Take three balls and decide who will start tossing. Each time a ball hits the imaginary corner, toss the next ball. Strive for consistency and accuracy of tosses. A toss-toss-toss-toss-toss-toss-toss-toss-toss-toss pattern will emerge with practice.

Stand alone

Practice tossing from left to right and back to yourself. Keep the tosses head high and wait for the ball to drop to your hand.

Go for two balls. Just as before, when the first ball hits the "imaginary corner" you should toss the other ball. Establish a pattern of toss-toss-pause, toss-toss-pause, toss-toss-pause.

Try three balls. Each time a ball hits the imaginary corner, release the next ball. Counting each toss helped me concentrate and determine progress.

Practice, practice, practice.

FACILITATOR NOTES:

People like to skip steps and start tossing three balls by themselves. Encourage everyone to "learn to crawl before they try to run." Part of the team building is the interaction with other people.

Many people have learned juggling by starting with scarves. People can learn to juggle scarves very quickly; however, the scarves fall so much slower than balls that most people must relearn the techniques when using the balls.

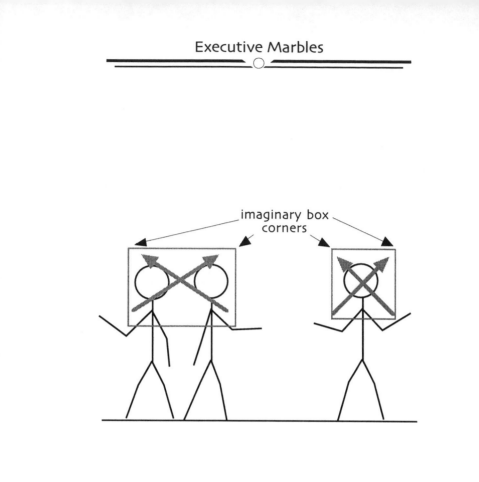

imaginary box
corners

Knowledge is Power

Knowledge is Power

PROPS:
15 things such as coins, paper clips, pens, etc.

OBJECTIVE:
Avoid being the last person to pick up the 15th object.

HISTORY:
Eric Johnson taught me this activity while we were on a break during a workshop. He said it helped him convince a company's decision maker that he might have valuable information to share with their people about how to work better as teams.

PREPARATION:
Lay 15 objects in a row on a table or on the floor

INSTRUCTIONS:
We will take turns taking away the objects from 1 to 15. You may take 1, 2, or 3 objects from the line of objects during each turn.

Try to get your competitor to pick up the last (or 15th) object.

FACILITATOR NOTES:
Use this activity with just two people or in pairs. As the person with the knowledge, it can be fun to get a group of pairs to play the game a few times and then play the winners yourself. The point is not to show off or get people frustrated. The point is that in many situations, having the right information makes you successful.

The following information is the knowledge that gives you the power to win (every time). Avoid giving people this information too soon or it will ruin the effect of the activity.

1) Always take the 10th object. (This is the first bit of knowledge to win.)
2) Always take the 6th object. (This is the second bit of knowledge to win.)
3) Always take the 2nd object. (This is the third bit of knowledge to win.)
4) If you go first, you can always win!

○○○○○⊘○○○⊘○○○⊘○

Masking Tape Activities

Masking Tape Activities

PROPS:
- Masking tape
- Other props as described in each activity

OBJECTIVE:
The intent of the following activity descriptions is to inspire ideas more than to give complete instructions for each activity. A person could devote a whole book to the use of masking tape; however, I wanted to hit the highlights and get the ideas in your heads now.

HISTORY:
As facilitators on-the-road we constantly look for ways to lighten our load. The following ideas originated when Mary and I were constructing our portable spider's web made of pipe and shock cord. The holes seemed too large for our group so Mary suggested I use masking tape to make the holes smaller. I proceeded to pull out some short ropes and stick them into place with the tape. Mary laughed and showed me what she meant by using the tape. She just pulled out a length of tape and stretched it across the hole. Wow, what a concept! Soon we were talking about making the whole web out of tape. A paradigm shift was born! The tape spider web works really well and you can rebuild it quickly if the tape breaks.

Spider Web
PREPARATION:
Make the spider web out of masking tape. Find a double-wide doorway or set two sturdy tables up on end approximately 7-10 feet apart. Tape the upper and lower lines first. Make the highest line about 6 feet and the lowest line about 1 foot off the floor. Place the

other lines as needed. Below are two examples.

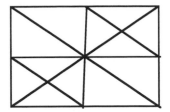 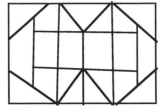

INSTRUCTIONS:
Go from one side of the web to the other without touching it. When someone uses an opening it cannot be used again. Be careful to support the person passing through the web to avoid falls or drops. If someone touches the web the team must start over with all the holes reopened.
Read more in *Cowstails and Cobras II* p.106, Kendall/Hunt Publishing

----

Islands
PREPARATION:
You will need a 6.5-foot 2X6, a 3.5-foot 2X6, a 3-foot 2X4, and masking tape.

Tape 3 squares on the floor to form the islands. Each square should be approximately 3 feet across and 7 feet from the other squares.

INSTRUCTIONS:
See the instructions for the Portable Islands in this book on page 150. The portable islands just got more portable. The activity takes longer to set-up with the masking tape, but it is lighter.

Nuclear Fence
PREPARATION:
Make the fence by stretching three lines of tape. Find a double-wide doorway or set two sturdy tables up

on end approximately 7-10 feet apart. Tape the upper line just higher than anyone can step over and lower line right at floor level. Stretch the third line between the upper and lower lines.

INSTRUCTIONS:
Get the whole team over the nuclear fence. No one may touch the fence in any way. Because of the radiation, the whole team will need to stay in physical contact with each other. Touching the fence or losing contact starts the activity over.
Read more in *Quicksilver* p.208, Kendall/Hunt Publishing

Photo Finish
PREPARATION:
Place two parallel lines of tape on the floor approximately 25 feet (8 m) apart.

INSTRUCTIONS:
Everyone needs to stand behind the starting line. When I say "Go", everyone will need to go to the finish line and cross it at exactly the same time. If anyone crosses the line sooner or later than anyone else it will cause you to start over. Crossing the finish line means breaking the imaginary plane above the tape.
Read more in *Feeding The Zircon Gorilla* p.114, Learning Unlimited

----

Bull Ring
PREPARATION:
You will need masking tape and a ring small enough to hold a tennis ball placed in it. Carefully unroll several strips of tape approximately 10 feet long. Lay them on the floor sticky side up like spokes on a wheel with the ring at the center of the wheel. Attach the tape to the ring by sticking the tape back to itself.

Place the tennis ball in the center.

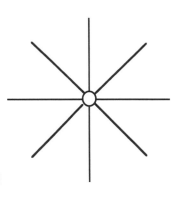

INSTRUCTIONS:
Each person should go to an end of each piece of tape and carefully lift the ball in the center without dropping it. Follow me across the room to deliver the ball into its container. Be careful not to pull too hard because the equipment is very fragile.

Bull ring usually uses string instead of tape. The tape offers additional challenges because it is fragile and one side is sticky.
Read more in *Teamwork & Teamplay* p.79, Kendall/Hunt Publishing

----

3-D Web
PREPARATION:
In a room or even outside tape a set of lines across the activity area from 10 to 20 feet square. Chairs, tables, and walls make good places to attach the web. Make the holes bigger than you think would be especially challenging. Start by taping around the perimeter and then across the area. Be sure to put lines too low to crawl under and the highest lines about 5 feet off the floor. Designate an entry and exit for the team.

INSTRUCTIONS:
As a team, make your way through the web without touching it. Touching the web can have terrible consequences (See Afflictions on page 40). Once you enter the web you must maintain physical contact with the team and no one may exit until everyone is

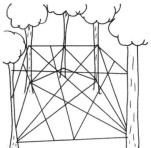

within the web area.
Read more in *Teamwork & Teamplay* p.175,
Kendall/Hunt Publishing

"Duct tape is like the Force. It has a light side, a dark
side, and it holds the universe together...."
Carl Zwanzig

Mouse Trap

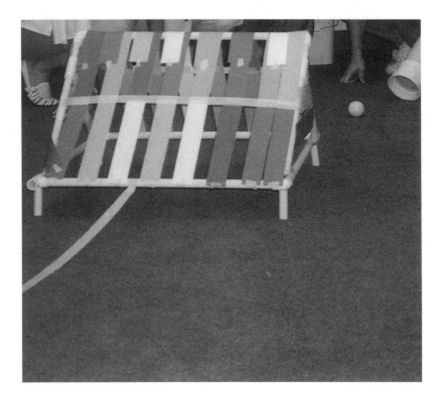

Mouse Trap

PROPS:
- All 1/2 inch (1.27 cm) PVC pipe
  - 6 - 2-foot pieces (.61 m)
  - 8 - 1-foot pieces (.3 m)
  - 20 - 3-inch pieces (7.63 cm)
  - 6 - Elbows
  - 6 - T fittings
  - 2 - Collars
- 10 sheets of paper
- 1 roll of tape
- 1 spool of thread
- 2 rubber bands
- 1 - PVC pipe 4 inches (10 cm) in diameter and 3.5 feet (1.07 m) long with a cap on each end (This is a good container to store the materials and roll/launch the ball through.)

OBJECTIVE:
Build a trap to capture a ball (mouse) launched from a pipe.

HISTORY:
Have you ever thought about building a better mouse trap? The mouse trap and the paper clip have been the marketing "bait" for many patent writing companies. People dream of inventing that one item that will change the world. In the spirit of invention, I made this activity so that there are many solutions. Some work well, others require miracles.

PREPARATION:
Place a mark on the floor that the ball will roll across. Inform the participants that the ball will roll over this mark on the floor.

INSTRUCTIONS:
Using the materials provided, construct a

mouse trap that will trap a ball (mouse) moving across the floor.

Parameters:
- No one can be within 15 feet (4.57 m) of the mouse when it is trapped.
- The trap must work regardless of which direction the mouse approaches.
- The trap must be a live-catch trap (no harpooning or crushing the mouse).
- The trap must not have holes large enough for the mouse to "escape".

You have 20 minutes to build your trap and catch the mouse. During that time you may make up to three trapping attempts.

SCENARIO:
Today is the Grand Opening of the first genetic super store, Clones-R-Us. You and your store team have made sure everything is clean and organized. Every item is ready to sell when, all of a sudden, you see a horrible sight. A laboratory mouse has escaped onto the showroom floor and the store opens in 20 minutes!

This mouse looks different than normal due to its enormous brain. It is an experimental I.L.R. (Intelligent Learning Rodent) developed only weeks ago. You must trap the mouse and remove it from the showroom before the store opens. Because ordinary mouse traps are useless to this "smart" mouse, you will have to build a better trap.

The other problem you face is the terrible bite the mouse can inflict. One bite from the mouse renders its victims stupid. Be sure to keep everyone at least 15 feet away from the mouse at all times.

FACILITATOR NOTES:

When the team is ready to trap a mouse move to a convenient location anywhere around the mark on the floor. You will want to stay a few feet from the mark so that people have some reaction time when you launch the mouse. To launch the mouse, set one end of the large pipe on the ground and roll the ball down through the pipe. You could just roll the ball by hand, but the speed of the roll can vary considerably from person to person. The pipe method produces a "catchable" mouse.

If the mouse escapes capture the team has two more tries within the 20 minutes.

Teams do not have to use all the materials. The photograph of the trap at the beginning of these instructions did not use 14 3-inch pipes, 4 1-foot pipes, 1 2-foot pipe, 2 T's, 2 collars, and 2 elbows.

WARNING:
Half Tennis Balls

WARNING:
Half Tennis Balls

In an attempt to be frugal and creative with our resources I recently took fifty tennis balls and carefully cut them in half with a sharp knife. My intent was to use them as "spots" or markers for any number of activities we do in our travels. They are light weight, easy to see, and compact. Little did I know what evil lay ahead for the innocent victims of improvisation.

It was the middle of a week-long training and we headed out to facilitate an activity from *Feeding The Zircon Gorilla* called On Target. Before the group started the high ropes course initiative, we had scheduled some time to warm up with a couple of low course activities. A facilitator (who will remain nameless) usually used hula hoops with his first event but I needed all the hula hoops we had, so I handed him a sack full of half tennis balls he might be able to use "somehow".

He facilitated a here-to-there activity called a nitro crossing. The participants simply swing on a rope across a designated area without touching the ground. Traditionally, there is a cup full of nitro glycerin (water) that also has to make the trip with no spills. Today, however, an added challenge emerged. Half of a tennis ball had to stay attached to each person's head as someone swung across the span. If a half ball fell off, everyone had to start over. So everyone used the suction from the tennis balls to stick them to their cheeks and foreheads. As each new person swung the distance someone in the group yelled, "ball check," to which the group responded by pumping their stuck half ball just a little more for security.

119

It is amazing how perfectly circular a half tennis ball can create a blood blister. By the grace of God, only three people had lasting marks on their heads. Unfortunately, one of those three had obtained great suction on his forehead that resulted in a deep, blood-red tennis ball sized blister. I understand that it was several weeks later that the color returned to normal.

I don't know what it is about the half tennis balls, but they somehow charm people to create a suction to their body. Just set them on a table and watch what people do. Hands, arms, legs, and foreheads seem to be the most popular places to stick them. Beware of their suction seduction.

Warning: Half Tennis Balls

OD = E²

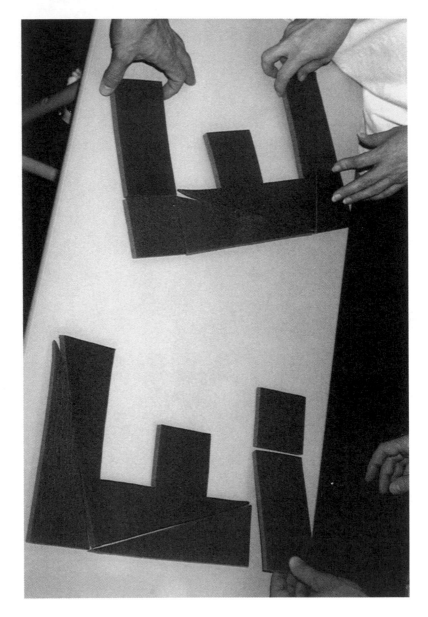

OD = E²

PROPS:
• 9 tanagram puzzles like the picture at the end of this activity

Make the pieces out of common materials like foam, wood, or cardboard. A good size for the pieces is 2 inches (5 cm) wide on each bar of the letter E. That would make the finished puzzle 6 X 10 inches (15 X 25 cm).

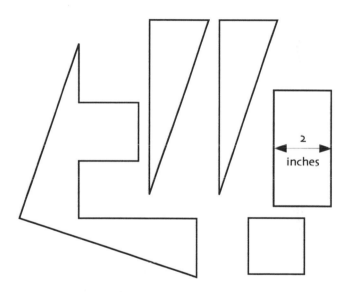

2 inches

OBJECTIVE:
Go through three puzzle activities that simulate common organizational stages.

HISTORY:
I was attending the AEE International Conference in Wisconsin when this activity came to me. I had been at a training pre-conference the week before. This activity emerged from the numerous discussions

we had about organizational development and why people do what they do in various situations.

PREPARATION:
Divide the puzzle pieces into 9 envelopes or zip-lock bags making sure there are enough pieces in each container for a complete E.

Distribute 2 bags to each of the 4 team areas and keep one bag until the beginning of round #2.

SCENARIO/INSTRUCTIONS:
E, Inc.
Once upon a time, someone created a great way to make E's with ease. The work went fast and the business grew quickly. Teachers bought E's for report cards, quality programs bought E's for excellence awards, and even e-mail was created. Business was going so well, but eventually competitors flooded the marketplace. Entrepreneurs grew E manufacturing facilities all over the country.

Round #1 - In 4 small teams, take no more than 1 minute to put together two capital E's with the 10 pieces provided.

The demand for E's did not decrease; however, the replication and complexity of effort made for limited profit. This industry needed experts. Anyone can become an expert if they specialize. So, that's just what happened. Each small business chose a special part of the E assembly (Essembly) process and began mass producing their part.

Round #2 - Each small team should take 2-3 minutes to choose one shape. Give it a name and create a reason for choosing that particular shape over the others.

(While the teams talk, give the pieces from the extra bag to one of the teams.)

In just a moment, you will be gathering your shapes so that you can corner the market. For example, if my team chose squares, we would gather all the squares, even those in other team's territories. The first small team to gather all the pieces of their shape will win the coveted leadership role for the next step in this activity.

RULZ: No one can keep other small groups from taking shapes from your area. Each person can carry only one piece at a time. This step is completed when each small team has all the different shapes--one shape per team. No kicking, hiding, or scratching is allowed. GO!

The reorganization of E making was not so easy. It took longer and required more effort than everyone thought it should. Lawyers stepped in to handle legal complaints and rule breaking.

As time passed, the experts discovered that making one shape and one shape only was pretty darned boring and risky business-wise. So, the mergers began. An empire made up of all the companies was formed.

Round #3 - Using all the pieces available, construct a solid square. The team that earlier gathered their shape the fastest has the leadership role. Complete this all-team merger within 15 minutes.

FACILITATOR NOTES:
Within each of the rounds there are a set of dynamics that tend to stand out.

In round #1 everyone is under a strict time constraint. They must move quickly and construct the entire product.

In round #2 everyone specializes to increase business. Some teams pick the same object and must negotiate until each team has a different set of shapes. Meanwhile, other teams may not have to negotiate and usually finish quickly and take leadership. Still other teams choose the triangle and soon realize there are twice as many to gather.

In round#3 the teams come together to cooperate on a common task even though they were just competitors. Motivation to work together often wanes. The product uses the same parts, but looks different.

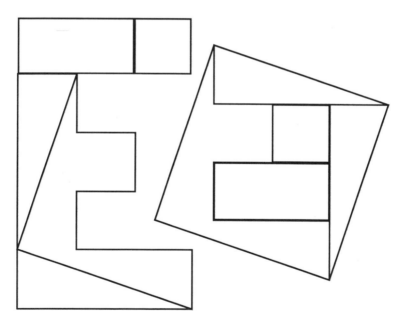

Onimod

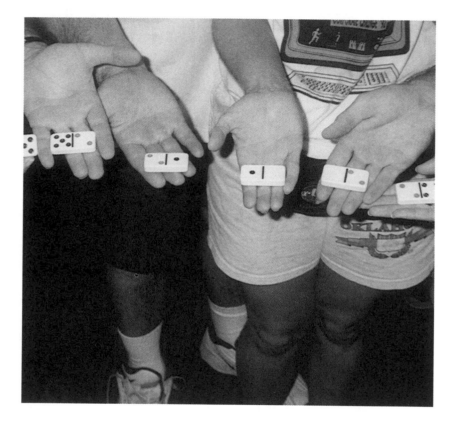

Onimod

PROPS:
- 1 set of dominoes or large laminated cards that look like dominoes

OBJECTIVE:
Onimod is a series of activities that you can facilitate using an ordinary set of dominoes. Below is a set of little known facts about dominoes that may come in handy for any number of activities. Onimod is domino spelled backwards.

<u>Use the following information to get people to network with most of the people in the room</u>.

Onimod Links
A link in dominoes occurs when two pieces have the same number of dots on an end. For example a 6-4 and a 4-2 link because they share the number 4. You match the ends together to start a line of domino pieces. The activities below use the concept of linking to get into a line or a circle next to someone you can introduce yourself to. The Onimod Links can take some time to solve unless a leader or coordinator emerges from the group.

There are 28 dominoes in a full set:
Give a piece to 28 people and they will always be able to link with the rest of the group. Everyone can also link in a circle. (Doubles may need to insert themselves between people who have already linked.)

Remove all the doubles (21 pieces):
Give the 21 pieces to 21 people and they will always be able to link with the rest of the group.

The 21 pieces will all link in a circle.

Remove the doubles and 6's (15 pieces):
The dominoes will link and always leave 2 pieces unlinked; also the end numbers will always read 0,1,2,3,4,5. The two unlinked people could be the "volunteers" for the next event.

Remove the doubles, 6's, & 5's (10 pieces):
Give the 10 pieces to 10 people and they will always be able to link with the rest of the group.

The 10 pieces will all link in a circle.

❖❖❖❖❖❖❖❖❖❖❖❖❖❖

Onimod Divisions
To divide a single group into smaller groups:
Give each person a domino and ask them to look at the highest number on their piece.

2 groups:
All the 6's, 5's, and blanks together	14
All the 4's, 3's, 2's, and 1's together	14

3 groups:
All the 4's and 3's together	9
All the 6's and 1's together	9
All the 5's, 2's, and blanks together	10

4 groups:
All the 6's together	7
All the 4's and 1's together	7
All the 5's and blanks together	7
All the 3's and 2's together	7

❖❖❖❖❖❖❖❖❖❖❖❖❖❖

Onimod Pairs
If you count all the dots on each piece and line them up in numerical order, you will end up with a bell-

shaped curve if you graph the frequency of the numbers.

Notice too that you can **pair people** by simply asking them to partner with someone so the sum of their dots equals 12. You will end with 14 pairs of people if you start with 28 people. If you have fewer people, just remove pairs of dominoes that add up to 12 until you have left the number of pieces you need.

Sum of dots	Frequency
0	1
1	1
2	2
3	2
4	3
5	3
6	4
7	3
8	3
9	2
10	2
11	1
12	1

Onimod Mixer

For a mixer: Ask everyone to meet and greet everyone else who has one of the same numbers on their domino. For example, if I have the 4-3, I'll network with everyone with a 4 and everyone with a 3 on their domino.

Everyone will meet 10 others if you eliminate the doubles and have 21 people.

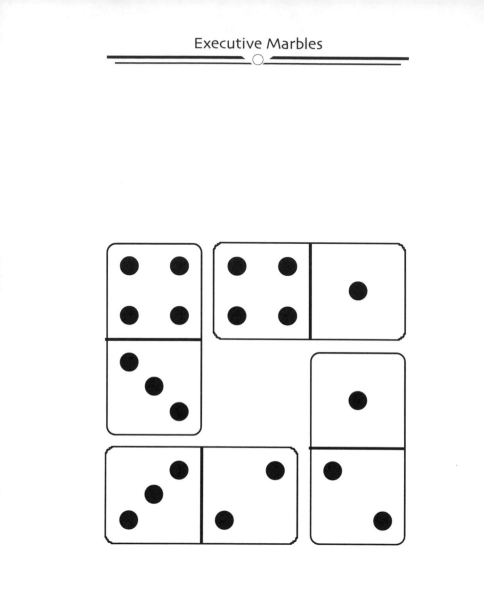

Paper Chute

Paper Chute

PROPS:
- 4 sheets of paper
- Tape
- 4 paper clips
- Scissors (optional)
- Felt tip markers (optional)
- Stop watch for the facilitator or timer

OBJECTIVE:
Design a structure that will free-fall as slowly as possible.

HISTORY:
Glen Olson conceived this variation of an object drop initiative while he was a training manager. What a great idea!

INSTRUCTIONS:
Construct a contraption that, when dropped 8 feet, will take the <u>longest</u> time to reach the ground. It must free-fall and be self-contained (no strings or other aids attached). You may only use the materials provided.

You will have three drops to get the best time. You can drop the same thing all three times or you can use up to three different designs.

The person timing your drop will count down, "3, 2, 1, drop!" The dropper will need to let go of the apparatus on "drop". The timer will start when you let go and will stop when the apparatus first touches the floor.

FACILITATOR NOTES:
If you have the time, try a best time out of three drops. It gives everyone a chance to

make the best of a sophisticated falling device.

When people start attempting to defy gravity they may ask very specific questions about the instructions. Here are some of the answers I often give: 1) You cannot bring in any extra materials, but you do not have to use all the materials. 2) No, you cannot lie on the floor and blow air to keep the object up longer; it is a free-fall. 3) Someone from your team can drop the creation, however, it must be dropped, not thrown.

Just in case you were wondering how fast an object might fall without any air resistance:

$$(x \text{ seconds})^2 = (\text{distance falling})/(.5 \times 9.8 \text{ m/s}^2)$$

For 8 feet (2.44 meters) the fastest free-fall is .71 seconds.

A personal best on this activity is 4.88 seconds. No tricks, no kidding.

VARIATIONS:

Consider prizes or recognition to the device that is most esthetically pleasing or the most interesting. Let people decorate their "thing" and market it to the group.

Another variation requires that each team use all the materials you provide.

Sample Flip Chart

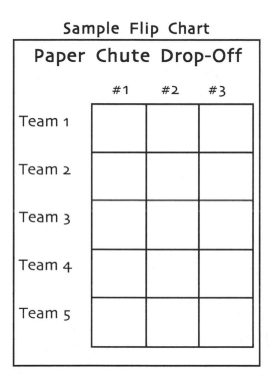

Paper Chute Drop-Off

	#1	#2	#3
Team 1			
Team 2			
Team 3			
Team 4			
Team 5			

Partner Stretches

Partner Stretches

PROPS:
None

OBJECTIVE:
Loosen muscles and get to know someone else in the room.

HISTORY:
John Irvin introduced me to these partner stretches a few years ago while we were working in Chicago. I have enjoyed using them in many of our programs. One great advantage to these stretches is that one facilitator can present to two people or a thousand.

INSTRUCTIONS:
Find a partner. . . someone you don't know very well. Quickly introduce yourself to your partner. Stand side by side.

Head rolls -
Relax your shoulders. Slowly and gently roll your head around clockwise. Be careful not to hyper-extend your head back. Now, switch directions and roll your head counter clockwise. Try not to fall down!

Side Stretch -
Stand side by side with your partner. Place your hand on your partner's closest shoulder. While both facing forward, reach your outside hand upwards and try to touch your partner's outside hand. Now bring your outside hands back down and reach down to touch the lowest point on your own outside leg.
(Repeat)

Switch sides with your partner and repeat the steps above.

Facing Stretch -
Stand facing your partner. Place your hands on their shoulders (not around their neck!!). Slowly bend at the waist and lower your head to form a table top with your upper body. Feel the stretch in the back and back of your arms. Slowly straighten up to your original position.

Quad Stretch -
Stand side by side with your partner. Place your hand on your partner's closest shoulder. While both facing forward, bring your outside foot up behind you and grab your foot. Use your partner for balance. Slowly pull your foot upwards and lean forward slowly. Straighten up and release your foot. (Repeat)

Switch sides with your partner and repeat the steps above.

Abs, Back, and Legs Stretch -
Stand back to back with your partner, then take a half step forward. Spread your feet shoulder width apart. Slowly reach your hands over your head and try to touch the fingers of your partner. Now slowly reach down through your legs and try to touch your partner's fingers. (Repeat)

FACILITATOR NOTES:
With any stretches, encourage people to move slowly and avoid bouncing. If you will do the stretches with the group they will follow your lead.

The quad stretch can be difficult for some people who have knee problems. Encourage people to do what will keep them healthy. Crashing to the floor is not allowed.

The abs, back, and legs stretch is a very good physical stretch and it is funny too. People will tend to spend little time bending down to touch fingertips so keep it moving. On the last time reaching between the knees I will say," Slowly reach down again between your knees. Grab your partner's hands and. . . . No, I'm just kidding," as if they were going to pull their partner out from between their legs.

The 6 Count at the beginning of the book is a good activity to follow the partner stretches.

Phone Tag

Phone Tag

PROPS:
- Flip chart paper or butcher paper
- Pens
- Sticky note pads
- Instruction and character page copies
- 2 regular six-sided dice

OBJECTIVE:
Solve a word puzzle using indirect communication similar to answering machines or e-mail.

HISTORY:
The phrase "phone tag" has haunted me for many years. I am not especially fond of calling people on the phone anyhow. Phone answering services have become so common, I thought we needed an activity that might test its strengths and weaknesses.

PREPARATION:
Make the call notes pages. Tape six flip chart papers or butcher paper pages to the walls in a room. Label each page with the name of a character in the activity.

Helen Waite	Oprah A. Tor	Buzz E. Signal	Kilroy Wazear	Nick L. Endime	R. E. Dial

Set up a command center. Mark a square around the station with tape or a rope. The command center needs a place to roll dice and a place for the facilitator to sit. The facilitator needs a copy of all the character descriptions and other activity rules to reference while the game plays. The facilitator also needs the

information on ANSWERS #1 & #2 (See below.).
ANSWER #1 needs to be on a separate slip of paper
so the participant can read through it. No papers
may leave the command center.

INSTRUCTIONS:
Divide the whole group into six small teams.

Pass out the character descriptions. Participants may
not show others the character descriptions you hand
out. Let the whole group know where the command
center is located and the following benefits and
hazards of using the command center:
• At the command center the facilitator can verbally
clarify instructions and help you understand the
puzzle.
• However, if ever there is more than one person at
the command center at a time, the whole system
goes down and all messages left on the call notes will
be lost (removed by the facilitator).

You will send messages by sticky note. You write
your message and place it on the call note pad of the
person you are trying to reach. Anyone can send
messages to anyone else unless otherwise instructed
in the character description.

There can be no direct communication except with
the people in your small group.
You may not read the contents of other character's
notes. No hand signals or touching (If you got hold
of someone it wouldn't be phone tag.)

Take a couple of minutes to get into character and
plan a personal strategy before we start the
messages.

Activity Template:
Copy or retype the following character descriptions,
instructions, and facilitator resources.

• •

Characters And Their Instructions

Helen Waite - You are slow to respond to messages because each time a person sends you a message, you must walk around the room to touch all the walls (really). This odd behavior has haunted you since the day you woke up in a large field in Kansas because of a practical joke.

There are less than eight letters in the puzzle. You know one of the letters is S.

o o o o o o o o o o o o o o o o o o o o o o o o o o o o o o o o o o o

Oprah A. Tor - You are a real networker. Most of your time is spent getting people to talk to each other. . . indirectly, of course.

You know that people can solve the puzzle if they will communicate with each other. The command center facilitator has two consecutive letters to the puzzle.

o o o o o o o o o o o o o o o o o o o o o o o o o o o o o o o o o o o

Buzz E. Signal - You send duplicate messages to everyone else each time you send anyone a message. You really want to make sure everyone knows what is going on.

You know one of the letters is E. The letters from the command center are not in alphabetical order. Kilroy's letter is close to Helen's.

○ ○

Kilroy Wazear - You call a lot just to chat. You fear you will be "left out" if you do not touch bases regularly.

You know one of the letters is L and Helen has the last letter.

○ ○

Nick L. Endime - You give short phone messages that are to the point. In fact, you never leave a message more than 5 words long.

You know one of the letters is A. R.E. Dial has a letter that is furthest from Helen's.

○ ○

R. E. Dial - You send every message twice just to make sure the person gets it.

You know one of the letters is M. The vowels are in alphabetical order.

● ●

Facilitator Command Center Resources

To get answer #1
You will have to work for a letter to the puzzle. Roll the dice. (If the number is eleven, roll again.) Take the total number that you roll and multiply it by 9. Add the two or three digits together and multiply by 3. Count that many letters into the <u>4th paragraph</u> of the joke below to find another letter to solve the puzzle.

One day a man came across a bottle washed up on the beach. He saw there was a cork in the bottle, so he pulled out the cork and instantly a genie appeared. He was very glad to be out of the bottle.

"I have been cramped in that bottle for years and now you have freed me," the genie bellowed. "As a measure of gratitude, I will offer you one wish."

The man was very excited and said, "I have always wanted to go to Hawaii, but I'm afraid of flying and boats take too long . . . please build me a highway to Hawaii so that I can drive there."

Thinking of all the cement, water, distance, and government regulations involved, the genie realized this wish was going to take too much effort on his part. So he said, "Think of another wish, <u>that</u> one uses too many resources . . . surely you can come up with a different wish!"

The man thought for a moment, then exclaimed, "I have always wanted to know how women think and what makes them do what they do. Give me understanding of women."

Without hesitation the genie said, "Would you like a two- or four-lane highway?"

⸰⸰

To get answer #2
You will have to work for a letter to the puzzle. Roll the dice and wait for a question. If you answer correctly, you will get a letter to the puzzle.

Odd Number Question: From the Bible story, how many animals of each species did Moses gather onto the ark?
Even Number Question: Approximately how many grooves are there on each side of a vinyl 33-rpm LP record?

If correct - Whisper to the person who rolled the dice: "B is the middle letter."

If incorrect - Whisper to the person who rolled the dice: "You are incorrect. Another character will have to try to get the right answer."

••••••••••••••••••••••••••••••••••

FACILITATOR NOTES:
The answer is a seven-letter word. Each character except Oprah has a letter and 2 letters are gathered at the command center.

There is the possibility of a system crash. All posted messages in the call notes come down and into the trash if more than one person at a time is in the command center. This allows you as a facilitator to avoid being mobbed.

Answer to #1
All answers are 9 X 3=27 and the 27th letter in the fourth paragraph is "R"

Answers to #2
ODD ANSWER: Zero - Noah put animals on the ark, not Moses.
EVEN ANSWER: One - It is a continuous groove spiraling toward the center.
SOLUTION: "Marbles"

VARIATIONS:
You can do this activity by computer on the internet. All you will need is a group of at least six people with e-mail capability.

Establish your command center before you begin. Get everyone's e-mail address saved into your computer's address book with the character names instead or their real names. Save the text from the activity you will be sending onto one document so that you can copy and paste some of the instructions to each person. Instead of rolling dice, just ask the person to pick a number from 1 to 12. This internet version is best played when everyone is at their computer, however, it can be played over the course of a few days if people are not constantly at their computers.

Portable Indoor Islands

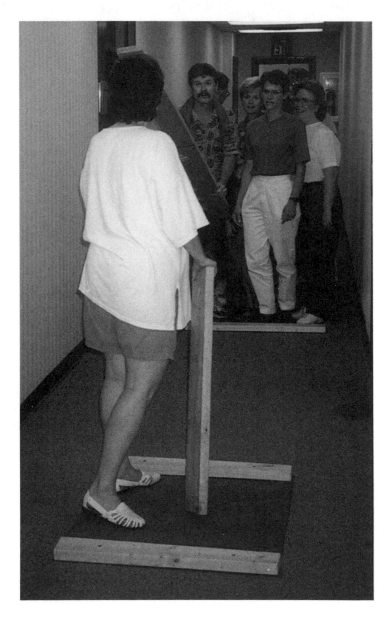

Portable Indoor Islands

PROPS:
- 1 - 6.5 foot (1.98 m) long 2X6 (5 X 15 cm) board - the board should have a permanent line dividing it in half. You may want to write a warning on the board as follows: **Warning, do not cross this line unless both ends are supported.** For practical reasons, this warning keeps people from breaking your long board with a "diving board" technique to solve the problem. (It also makes the problem more challenging.)
- 1   3.5-foot (1.07 m) long 2X6 (5 X 15 cm) board
- 3 squares of carpet approximately 2 to 4 feet (.61 to 1.22 m) across
- 4   2X4 (5 X 10 cm) boards the same length as your carpet squares

OBJECTIVE:
Using the long board and the short board, get the whole group from the first island to the last island without anything touching the ground.

HISTORY:
If you are familiar with the "islands" or "mountain tops" initiative, you will already understand how to use the portable islands.

Islands are usually found outside on a low ropes course. Normally there are 3 wooden platforms (sometimes permanently fixed to the ground) spaced approximately 7 feet from each other and situated in a row of three platforms or an "L" of three platforms. The islands not attached to the ground are "portable", but only if you have strong muscles and a lot of car space. I think you will find the islands below much less of a strain.

I try not to think about how many times I have strained to put three giant boxes in my car. Now I can roll all three islands and tuck them under my arm.

PREPARATION:
Place the carpet squares on the floor leaving approximately 7 feet between them. (6 to 8 inches longer than your longest board) If someone has not already attached the 2X4s, stick the 2X4s on the carpet squares as shown in the diagram on the next page. I use wood-to-wood connector bolts because they are sturdy and screw in flush, but staples, glue, deck screws, or nails will work.

INSTRUCTIONS:
Get the team over to the last island without touching the floor with anything in the process. Your only resources besides yourselves are these two boards. Be aware of the warning on the long board. Any contact with the floor will have dire consequences. You may not move the islands. No long jumps.

SCENARIO:
Because of the liquids you drank today, you have all shrunk to the size of a grain of rice. You find yourself trapped on an old computer keyboard. Notice the three keys in front of you and the paper clip and nail file lying on the first key. Also notice the circuit board that the keys are resting on. The circuit board is charged with electricity and should be avoided at all costs. One touch to the circuit board and terrible things could happen! (Fried rice!)

Your only hope for freedom is at the farthest key. By chance or miracle, the weight of the entire team is just enough to press the key and turn off the computer. . . and the electrical charge.

Remember that paper clips and nail files are great electrical conductors.

TOP VIEW

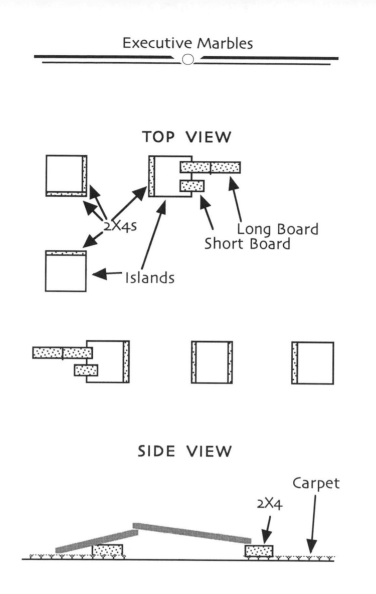

2X4s

Long Board
Short Board

Islands

SIDE VIEW

Carpet

2X4

FACILITATOR NOTES:

People often touch the floor by unintentionally hanging their feet off the edge of the carpet because the carpet does not create much height.

Mouse traps set between the islands add a challenging effect.

It is a good idea to ask one or two people to help spot each person walking across the boards. Spotters put themselves in a position to keep someone from falling to the ground and hurting themselves, however, spotters do not touch the crosser unless it is for safety. Spotting generally occurs because the two boards slip to the side, move, or fall unexpectedly.

VARIATIONS:
Add 2 hula hoops and a 10 foot piece of rope to the props. The team needs to stay in physical contact with each other to avoid afflictions.

Quadrapus

Quadrapus

PROPS:
- 2 Kernmantle ropes approximately 50 feet (15 m) long
- 4 Pairs of different colored bandannas or markers
- 2 Carabiners
- 5 to 10 feet (1.5 to 3 m) of webbing or strong rope

OBJECTIVE:
Four small teams compete or cooperate to untangle their ropes and capture their flag.

HISTORY:
Steve Balsters created this team activity. It is a good example of cooperation or competition within a connected system.

PREPARATION:
The preparation instructions seem fairly long for this activity, but it actually takes 15 minutes to set-up once you understand the concept.

To prepare for this activity you need to tie the ropes, measure the distances to the flags, and tangle the ropes.

Locate a grove of trees or a location with obstacles (like columns).

Tie - Tie a small loop in the middle of each rope with a butterfly knot or other similar knot.

Tie webbing around a tree in the center of the grove, then attach the kernmantle ropes to the webbing with the carabiners. (See illustration)

At each of the four ends of the rope, tie a

loop big enough for each small team to hold on. Make sure the knot will not slip.

Measure - Take each rope end and pull the rope straight away from the tree attachment. Pull it firmly to fully extend the rope and place a flag approximately 6 feet beyond the end. Mark the end of the rope with its matching flag so the group can identify it as their rope and flag.

Tangle - Take each rope and have fun tangling it around the trees and the other ropes. (See illustration) Remember that the team will have to follow the rope's path to untangle it so do not thread the ropes through a hole that no one can get through, or over a limb you do not want everyone to climb.

INSTRUCTIONS:
Divide the group into 4 small teams.

Ask each small team to choose one of the 4 loops at the end of the ropes. Ask them to grab the rope and listen to the rules.

RULZ:
• Each team's objective is to capture the flag that matches the one tied to your rope.
• You must move no faster than a walk.
• Everyone must maintain a grip on their rope loop with the same hand at all times.
• Knots tying the rope end and the ropes to the tree cannot be untied (this includes the carabiners).
• Avoid potential rope burns by staying alert to rope against skin contacts. Anyone can yell "freeze" if something becomes unsafe.

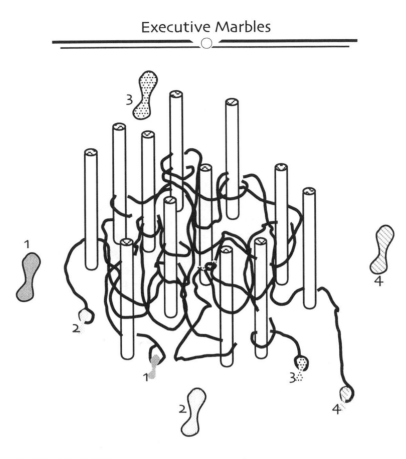

SCENARIO:

You are on a corporate mission to free your company from the government restrictions placed on it over the last few years. Until you reach the goal (bandanna), everyone on your team must remain firmly attached to the restrictive tether to avoid further restrictions. If you are able to comply with the restrictions <u>and</u> reach your goal, the company will have satisfied its obligations and be free to move beyond its current restrictions. (If you capture the flag, you can let go of the rope.)

Unfortunately, a few other companies are in the same situation, yet they have different goals to reach before they are free.

159

Free your company sooner than the others and you will certainly have a competitive advantage. Note that unsafe practices will cause OSHA to regulate the entire industry, so be alert to the safety of your team and the safety of other teams.

FACILITATOR NOTES:

There are several approaches people make to this activity. Most often it is the "untangle ourselves and ignore everyone else" strategy. Sometimes a team focuses on the competition by trying to tangle their rope or block their path while still reaching their own goal. Others try to cooperate with the other teams until the last moments of the activity.

The truth is that even if a team untangles completely, they may not be able to reach their flag if another team has taken up the slack at the webbing loop. It can come down to a four-way tug-of-war.

I have never had any troubles with the ropes injuring anyone, but it is a good idea to watch carefully for potential problems. Obviously, no one should wrap a rope around their hands, neck, etc.

VARIATIONS:

When the activity and discussion are complete ask the teams to prepare the ropes for the next group to do Quadrapus. Watch how much effort they put into tangling the ropes. Then (this is pretty sneaky) ask them to do the activity again.

Rock Paper Scissors

Rock Paper Scissors
Cycles: Separate but connected

Scissors cut Paper
Paper covers Rock
Rock breaks Scissors

Earth controls Water
Water puts out Fire
Fire burns Earth

Colonel Sanders eats Chicken
Chicken eats Worm
Worm eats Colonel Sanders (He passed away.)

Bear eats Fish
Fish eats Mosquito
Mosquito eats Bear (albeit a little at a time)

Elephant scares Cat
Cat scares Mouse
Mouse scares Elephant

Giants squash Elves
Elves outmaneuver Wizards
Wizards cast spells on Giants

Cowboy uses Clown
Clown tricks Bull
Bull gores Cowboy

Saul runs from Goliath
Goliath dies from David
David hides from Saul

Elephant crushes Man
Man crushes Ant
Ant brings down Elephant (crawls up nose)

Ah leads to So
So leads to Ko
Ko leads to Ah

Do-Re-Mi-Fa-Sol-La-Ti and it brings us back to Do

PROPS:
• Spot markers or chairs for each person plus one extra
• Cards with character names or symbols on them (optional)

OBJECTIVE:
Rearrange the group so that the people with the same names are together.

HISTORY:
I have always been interested in cycles that, for the most part, go in one direction. Maybe it is my need for structure and predictability. . . or maybe not. The collection of one-way cycles came from a variety of sources. For example, the Elephant, Man, Ant cycle comes from an African folk tale.

PREPARATION:
Place enough markers or chairs in a circle for everyone plus one extra.

I like to teach people non-verbal hand signals for each of the characters, but other people like to make name cards. If you have cards, pass them out once everyone has taken a seat.

INSTRUCTIONS:
You could use the following instructions for a group of 9 to 30 people.

"Everyone take a seat. Has everyone played Rock,

Paper, Scissors? We are about to do an activity that has similar dynamics. Each of you will be assigned a name that will determine who you dominate. The object of the activity is to end up sitting in a group next to everyone who has the same character name as you."

"Now there are some restrictions to how you may rearrange yourselves. 1) You may slide over into an empty seat next to you or 2) you may skip over <u>one</u> person next to you to sit in an empty seat. The only way you can skip a person is if you are dominant over them. 3) No one can go across the circle to take a different seat. 4) Only one person may move at a time."

"So let's find out who is who so you will know where you rank. Let's go around from person to person with Colonel Sanders, Chicken, Worm, Colonel Sanders, Chicken, Worm, etc. So who do you dominate? Colonel Sanders eats Chickens, Chickens eat Worms, and Worms eat Colonel Sanders (because he is no longer with us; he's dead). So a Chicken can skip over a Worm to take an empty seat, but Colonel Sanders cannot skip over a Worm."

"So you will know who is who, since you probably cannot tell just by looking at them, we need to establish some signals that show who is who. The Chickens should put their hands to their shoulders to form wings. The Worms should hold their hands together and stick out an index finger like a worm coming out of an apple. The Colonels should put an index finger under their nose like a mustache and a fist under their chin like a goatee beard. This way there will be no mistaking who is who."

"The object is to get all the Colonel Sanders together, all the Worms together, and all the Chickens together. Go!"

SCENARIO:

Who would have believed that you could have made this happen? Representatives from three nations are meeting for a peaceful end to a long-term conflict. Each county is a world leader in one area of the global market and each country is dependent on another to maintain its status.

Everything is going well until you realize the seating arrangements for the meeting have been mixed. You wanted people sitting by country around the table and just the opposite has occurred. You must act quickly to avoid an international incident. You leave your own seat open and ask the assembly to tolerate an exercise in seeing things from another's perspective.

You ask the group to move one at a time (so as not to start a panic) into an empty seat. Any person to the left or right of the open seat may slide over to it. Only a dominant country's representative can skip over a dependent country's representative to sit in an open seat. You ask them to change positions until each country's representatives are seated next to each other.

FACILITATOR NOTES:

When the group has completed their task, see if they can do it again more quickly. . . or silently. . . or with the fewest moves. The group may be able to complete the task while everyone holds his breath!

Usually a leader emerges to direct traffic. Sometimes the group will "spin its wheels" for a while until they decide who will end where.

All the cycles in the list above are one-way. Of course there are debatable exceptions just like the classic news headline "Man Bites Dog". Nevertheless, the cycles give a common sense structure to the activity.

VARIATIONS:

Try the cycles on the classic TP Shuffle activity. Everyone stands in a line on a telephone pole laid on the ground. The facilitator moves down the line assigning the character names, "Rock, Paper, Scissors, Rock, Paper, Scissors, Rock. . . ." Then the group tries to rearrange themselves so that each character type is standing together.

Like the classic activity, no one can touch the ground. A difference from the classic is that only the dominant character can take the initiative in the crossing. For example a Rock can pass by the Scissors because it is dominant between the two, but the Rock must be passed by the Paper.

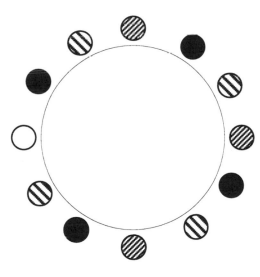

Stringin'em Along

Stringin'em Along

Warning: Do not use this activity unless you have a clear working knowledge of the equipment used for the activity (i.e., tying knots, belaying, attaching carabiners to safety anchors, using rope pulleys, harnessing). The activity may be perceived as risky. However, if it is properly prepared and operated the actual safety risk is minimal.

PROPS:
- 4 rope pulleys
- 14 carabiners - 4 of them attach the pulleys to the poles or trees
- 4 kernmantle ropes to belay the hovering participant
- At least 5 seat harnesses, preferably one for each person
- 1 chest harness
- Task materials - such as PVC pipes, hula hoops, balls, cones, blocks, ropes, etc.

OBJECTIVE:
This activity needs thirteen or more people involved to make it work safely. The team communicates together to maneuver one of its members above the ground to accomplish a task. The dynamics of this activity demonstrate the needs and necessities of a support group helping someone in the "spotlight" to do their work.

HISTORY:
A few years ago there was a request from our customers to create more of a team emphasis on high ropes course events. This activity is similar to "Lines of Communication" from *Feeding The Zircon Gorilla*. Instead of dropping a ball in a bucket, we "giant sized" the activity and the team

maneuvers a person suspended by climbing ropes. It is a unique feeling to be the person being held by so many people. In our initial tests of the activity we were lifting people 40 feet into the air!

PREPARATION:
Secure each pulley and rope to a high safety cable or eye bolt at each pole so that the pulley will not slide on the cable. Run the rope through the pulley. Tie a bowline on a bight at both ends of the ropes.

Use 2 carabiners at each belay end of the rope to attach to 2 people's harnesses in each small group. (The other person will hold on to the belayers' belts.) Use 2-3 carabiners to attach the four ropes to the back of the person being lifted.

Tie a string diagonally across the playing area and approximately 8 feet high. Place the materials for the task in the playing area.

INSTRUCTIONS:
Split the group into 4 smaller groups. The 4 groups will lift one person by using separate belay systems.

The hovering team member will collect materials to accomplish a task such as retrieving and dunking 3-4 balls into a hula hoop attached to a support or placing pipes on the ground to spell a word.

Rulz:
• No one may contact the ground or dividing string in the play area.
• At least 3 people must be supporting each rope.
• Only the person hanging may touch the materials.
• The person being lifted must begin outside the play area.

SCENARIO:
You have been selected for this assignment based on

your skills at working together. Your mission is to send a message across enemy lines. Our allies have been instructed to look at a specific location to get their orders in the form of a code word. The code word you will be sending is "TEAM".

The message location is heavily monitored by highly sophisticated electronic security systems including a pressure sensitive ground alarm and an aerial trip wire. You will need to write the message in large block letters with the materials lying at the site (13 2-foot sticks of PVC pipe). You must carefully lift a person above the ground using ropes and guide the hovering person to the writing materials where he or she will pick up one or two pieces. The rest of the group will need to lift the person over the trip wire and lower him or her on the other side to carefully lay the writing materials on the ground in the form of the code word. A person may carry only two pieces of the writing material at a time. Once the materials are set on the ground, the teams must guide the person out of the area and relieve him or her with another carrier. A carrier may go into the secured area only once because we fear that there is a high concentration of nuclear radiation at the site.

Touching the ground or the trip wire can have terrible consequences for the carrier even if the rope touches the trip wire. Another crew has already set up your safety equipment so that you can complete your mission. Remember to use your harnesses. Good luck.

FACILITATOR NOTES:
A quick physics lesson- The more vertical the ropes from the hovering person to the anchors at the pole or trees, the easier it is to lift them. In order for a person to be held off the ground while the ropes are horizontal requires a force of 28 times their weight.

Try to attach your rope pulleys as high as you can and do not separate the anchors from each other by too far. An activity area of 20 by 20 feet with anchors approximately 35 feet in the air are ideal. Many ropes courses have poles or trees already in this type of setting.

Consequences to the carriers, such as blindness, can last until after they have had to be a rope holder for a while.

Support each person while they are first being lifted to ensure that they do not swing and hit the ground at the start. The other participants can perform this role if you have enough people. Monitor safety throughout the activity. Are people paying attention? Is everything hooked? Are the ropes untangled?

VARIATIONS:
This activity has worked well using only 3 ropes. The activity instructions are the same; however, the force needed to lift the person in the middle is greater.

At the belayer's end of each rope you can attach a set of lobster claws to split the load and make it more comfortable for the lifters.

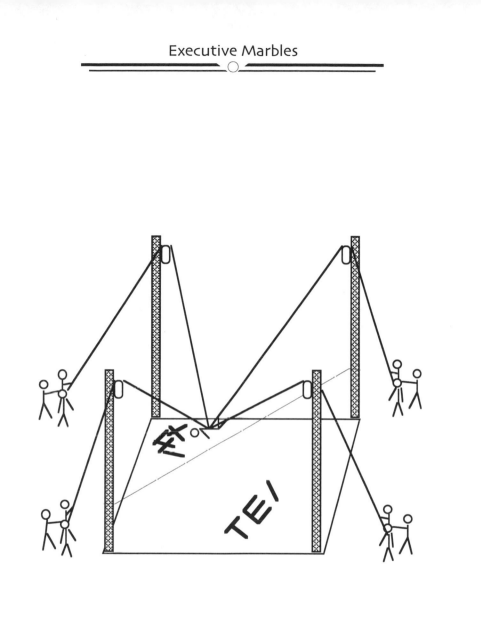

Carabiner Song

Sung to the tune of the
Oscar Mayer wiener song

Oh I wish I were a steel carabiner,
that is what I'd truly like to be.
Cause if I were a steel carabiner,
everyone would hang around
with me!

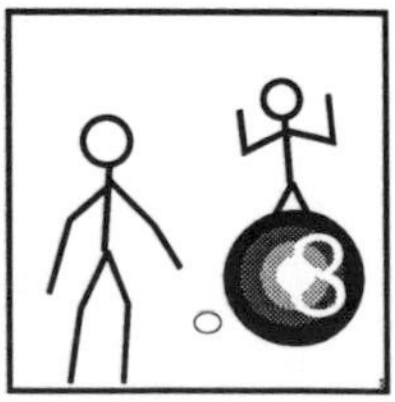

Thinking Outside The Box

Thinking Outside The Box

PROPS:
- Masking tape. Ideally you should have one roll of tape for each group of 3-4 people. However, groups can share tape.

OBJECTIVE:
Get to know other people quickly in a group and creatively situate everyone into a small space by moving from square area to square area meeting different people.

HISTORY:
Creativity is a valued commodity in businesses these days. This activity borrows the concept of other "vanishing resources" games, but adds the twist of literally thinking outside the box to solve the problem. It also makes for a good icebreaker. I experienced a similar exercise in 1995 led by Michael Gass.

PREPARATION:
Establish a facilitated process in which the whole group discusses what keeps them in their "boxes" and how they get out of the routine or status quo. List the key points on flip chart pages as the discussion progresses.

INSTRUCTIONS:
Quickly divide into small groups of 2 to 4 people.

Take the masking tape that is being handed out and make a square on the floor approximately 3 or 4 feet across so that everyone in your small group can easily stand inside the square. When you

finish, stand in the square and take a moment to introduce yourself to the rest of your group. We will be doing this for several rounds.

Now, when everyone has both feet on the floor inside the squares, I will yell "change" and you should quickly disband from your small group, find another square to stand in and introduce yourself to your new group members.

I will not say "change" again until everyone's feet are inside a square.

FACILITATOR NOTES:
Say "change" when everyone has both feet inside a square and they have had just enough time to meet their group.

If none of the groups have made a box small enough for the group size, take a moment to make a box for yourself that you can use as the final box.

After two rounds, start removing a square from the floor during each new round. Obviously, there will start to be more people in each area. The next round cannot start until everyone is in a square. Finally, all but one of the squares will be taken up off the floor and the last box seems too small to accommodate everyone without people "getting out of the the box" with their bodies.

Usually the group solves their space problem by sitting on the floor and resting their feet inside the square instead of struggling for balance while trying to stand.

When the group finishes the activity, debrief and add to the lists of comments the group started earlier.

If you can, avoid putting masking tape on a tile or

linoleum floor. The tape sticks too well. You could use ribbon or plastic marking strips taped at the corners. Then there would be less tape to remove.

How big or small should the last box be? I just make a good guess. Imagine everyone placing just their shoes on the floor inside a square. Some shoes may be up on their heels. That's the size!

VARIATIONS:
You can direct the discussion of the small groups to a specific topic. The following are a few topics we have used:
Discuss what you plan to do when you retire.
You have just won the lottery. How will it change your life?
The things I like most about my job are. . .

The Tick

The Tick

PROPS:
- 1 uniquely decorated clothespin
- 5 slips of paper with conditions written on them

OBJECTIVE:
Avoid being the last person with the tick when it is called for.

HISTORY:
Mike Spiller introduced this activity to me in 1997. He said the game was called "The Curse". That name has some bad connotations for some people, so we renamed it after the object that is hidden or stuck to people. In a pre-conference gathering the Tick gained popularity and actually carried over into another conference five states away.

PREPARATION:
Make a Tick from a clothespin. Decorate it so that it would be hard to duplicate. Keep the decoration light weight but bright enough to see easily.

Cut out the prepared conditions at the end of these instructions or create your own. Be sure one of the conditions is positive. The positive condition gives a victim some glimmer of hope as he or she walks up to select a slip of paper.

INSTRUCTIONS:
We are beginning an ongoing activity that will continue until the last time we gather as a group. I have in my hand a tick. It is really a decorated clothespin that I will hide on someone or their personal property. That person may find it and hide it on someone else. When we call for a "tick check," whoever has it will need to come up to the front of the

181

room to choose a slip of paper that will instantly diagnose the strange condition they have contracted from the tick.

Here is an example of how a tick check will proceed: I will call for the tick and say that I had the tick and I gave it to John. John will stand up and say that he found it in his shirt pocket and he gave it to Sheri. Sheri will stand and say she found it on her purse strap and she gave it to Bob. Bob will stand and say something like "Shoot, I don't know where it is." Bob would come up and draw a slip of paper and read his condition. The condition would be in effect immediately. Sheri would tell Bob where she hid the tick. Bob would then hide the tick on someone else before the next tick check. Bob's condition would last until the next tick check unless the condition stated otherwise. When I called for the next tic check, Bob would start the hunt for the tick.

Rulz:
- You may only hide the tick on someone if you know their name.
- You must hide the tick in a public area. In other words, stay out of luggage, inside closed purses, locked vehicles, etc.
- When the tick check is officially called, the tick sticks where it is. It is too late to pass it on.
- If you find the tick, remember where you found it.
- Once you have contracted a strange condition you are immune to further afflictions. In other words, no one can be caught with the tick more than once. If they are, the next to last carrier is afflicted.

FACILITATOR NOTES:
This activity is intended for larger groups that will be together for more than a day. Conferences of less than 200 people have a great time with the activity.

Paranoia will set in after a few hours of the game. People everywhere will be feeling their clothes, regularly looking at backpacks and purses, and turning to friends for visual tick surveillance. Just a strange glance will start them looking.

Keep the slips of paper with you and pull them out when you call for the tick. Once a condition is used, eliminate it from the future choices.

On the last tick check, get the tick from the victim or you may get it back months later at a surprise tick check in front of hundreds of people. Believe me I know!

Tick Conditions

- You must run around the room three times saying, "I'm okay, you're okay!"

- Once a minute for the next 10 minutes you must say a loud "Yes!"

- You must do a magic trick for us right now.

- A person near you at the time of the tick check must serve you like your own personal maid or butler until the next tick check.

- You must lead the group in singing the Oscar Mayer wiener song.

- You must shake hands with anyone who talks to you.

- You must look eight inches to the right of anyone you are speaking to.

- You must maintain physical contact with someone whenever two or more people are in the room with you.

"The Audience"

Urban Zip

Urban Zip

Warning: Do not use this activity unless you have a clear working knowledge of the equipment used for the activity (i.e., tying knots, belaying, attaching carabiners to safety anchors, using rope pulleys, harnessing). The activity may be perceived as risky. However, if it is properly prepared and operated the actual safety risk is minimal.

PROPS:
- 2 static climbing ropes
- 1 rat tail or lanyard 2 feet (.6 m) long
- 5 Steel carabiners
- A helmet for the zipper
- Seat harness for each zipper
- 1 Dynamic belay for the climbers
- 1 Static attachment for the facilitator up top
- A ladder (optional)

OBJECTIVE:
Safely slide down ropes from a tall tree or building.

HISTORY:
Joel Cryer introduced me to this activity at the same conference in Louisiana where we initially tested the hot air balloon activity. We needed a zip line for a workshop and did not have a ropes course close by. The Urban Zip made a great portable high event. Since that time we have used the Urban Zip for a variety of ages and sizes of people.

PREPARATION:
For this activity, you will be in search of the ideal tree or an ideal building. The ideal tree has limbs to climb all the way to the launch site. It also has a nice large branch for you and the participant to sit on. The trunk is sturdy and at least 10 inches in diameter

where you will attach the zip line ropes. On a building the ideal location will have a strong place to attach the zip line ropes and a place to launch from just underneath the ropes. Of course, in both instances you will want a clear, flat path between the top of the zip and the two belay teams.

Tie the top of the zip line. The zip line itself will need to be at a 45° to 30° angle from the ground. If it is 45° then the participant will zip out as far as he had to climb. Tie a bowline on a bight or a figure eight on a bight in one of the ropes. Wrap the rope twice around the tree. Situate the rope so that the knot is on the same side as the zip. Clip a carabiner through the knot loop(s), over the zip line, and over the first wrap on the tree. The rope should be secure enough not to slide down the tree when the participant adds his weight. Now, attach the other rope in the same way just above or below the first rope. Each rope will use approximately 10 feet for this attachment.

Clip two steel carabiners side-by-side over both zip line ropes. Attach a lanyard or "rat tail" to the two steel carabiners. Clip another carabiner to the other end of the lanyard. This lanyard will hold the participant to the zip lines.

Back on the ground, tie a loop approximately 6 feet in diameter at the end of each zip line. Use a bowline with a follow through or a figure eight on a bight with a 6-foot loop. Each rope will use approximately 18 feet for this attachment. The belay teams will stand snugly inside these loops to support the weight of the person zipping.

Rig a dynamic belay system for the participants climbing the tree or ladder. Also, rig a secure attachment for the facilitator who will stay at the top to connect each participant to the zip lines.

INSTRUCTIONS:

This is a people powered zip line. Those who want will have an opportunity to slide down the rope to the ground. This zip decent is not very fast, but it is a unique experience.

Divide into two groups. Each group should have a minimum of 5 people. Step into the rope circles. Hold the rope on your back at your waist. It may be a little crowded. We will be tightening the zip line ropes by pulling back as a person zips down the lines. The rope circle will stay the same size. The person's weight will pull you, so stand in a strong position. The "V" formed by the two zip lines will determine how quickly the person will slide down the line. The further apart the two belay teams are from each other the more slowly the person will slide. In fact we can stop the zipper at any time by keeping the line tight and moving further apart from the other belay team. You are the safety for the zipper. Keep the lines tight and focus on the zipper. When the person reaches the ground, loosen the rope and let the person detach the safety line.

To get the safety line back to the top, both teams should pull their ropes in opposite directions perpendicular to the zip line path. This will pull the safety line to the facilitator in the tree. Another way to get the safety line back into place is to detach it and let the next zipper carry it into place and reattach it to the zip lines.

Those who are zipping have some responsibilities. Carefully climb to the launch site and let the facilitator connect you to the zip lines. Avoid holding the zip lines and avoid getting clothing or hair near the carabiners. When you are ready to zip yell, "Zipping!" Wait for both belay teams to yell, "Zip On!" Then scoot off the launch site and slide down the ropes.

FACILITATOR NOTES:

As with most events similar to this one, the first person to do the event sets the tone for the rest of the group. Pay close attention to the details of the set-up and the understanding by the participants.

The first person to go should not be the heaviest person. Let the group experience the event with a lighter and more controllable person first. The participants need this first experience to learn what small adjustments to make. How tight is the rope? How fast will the zipper travel? Do I need to pull harder or not as hard? Will this work?

Do not let the belay teams stand right next to each other. The zipper could slide down the ropes too quickly and hit the belay teams.

If you have gone to all the trouble of finding a tree, climbing a tree, and tying everything together, you probably want to make sure you have enough rope in the end. A zip line attached 30 feet off the ground will need a maximum of 59 and a minimum of 43 feet plus approximately 28 feet for the knots and attachments for each rope. Below is a diagram showing how long the ropes need to be.

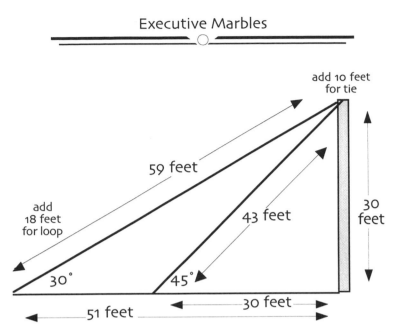

add 10 feet for tie

add 18 feet for loop

59 feet

43 feet

30 feet

30°

45°

51 feet

30 feet

The materials list asks for static ropes. You can safely do this activity with dynamic ropes; however, the zipper will not go as far because of the extra stretch in the rope.

VARIATIONS:

Instead of simply zipping down the lines, let the team and zipper shoot for some targets with water balloons or balls. Try an "On Target" event (See *Feeding The Zircon Gorilla*, p. 90) and spread targets so that the belay teams have to move the zipper to the sides in order to hit some of the targets.

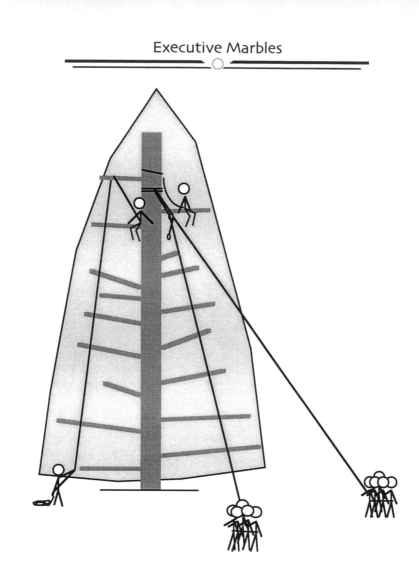

Water Towers

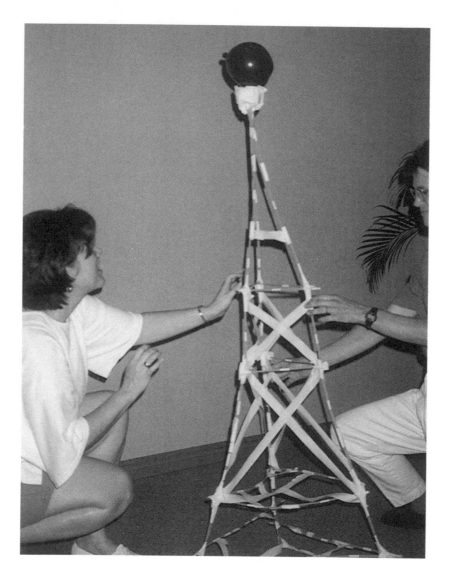

Water Towers

PROPS:

For each team of 4-6 people
- 12 ounce (340 g) package of spaghetti per team
- 1 water balloon approximately 4 inches (10 cm) in diameter
- 1 roll of masking tape

OBJECTIVE:

Build a water tower as high as possible out of spaghetti and tape.

PREPARATION:

Carefully fill a balloon with water until it is approximately 4 inches in diameter. Place the props on the floor or on tables so that each team will have plenty of room to begin construction.

INSTRUCTIONS:

Using only the supplies provided, build the tallest, free-standing, self supporting tower that will support the water balloon at the top.

You will have 35 minutes to complete the task.

SCENARIO:

Many people are unaware that in this part of the country fresh water can be very hard to come by. The water that is available has to be pumped up several hundred feet from the Ersatz Aquifer.

Knowing that you all would be here to work on building teams, the "locals" have asked us for your help to design a new water tower for the area. They want us to build a model that meets their building requirements.

The tower needs to be as tall as possible to increase the water pressure in the pipes.

The model that we are building can use only 12 ounces of dry spaghetti and one roll of masking tape as building materials.

The tower must be free-standing and self-supporting.

Finally, the tower must support the water for which it is being built. (Show a water balloon.)

Great rewards will be given to the team that builds the tallest tower that meets the requirements above.

You have 35 minutes to build the tower. Go!!!

FACILITATOR NOTES:

When we started using these materials for teams to build towers we used only masking tape and spaghetti. The towers would go higher and higher, but rarely, after the time expired, did a tower stand more than 18 inches. It seems that most people built their structures for quick height and little stability. As a result, most towers crumbled to the floor before the end of the activity.

We added the water balloon to the supplies to add an extra challenge to a team we facilitated. It was interesting to discover how differently each small group approached the task. The weight of the balloon caused them to focus on the strength of the structure as well as its height. As a result, every tower stood and was over 3 feet tall! The same dynamic has occurred with subsequent teams. Given a greater challenge, each team created greater results with the same building materials.

8

Water Fall

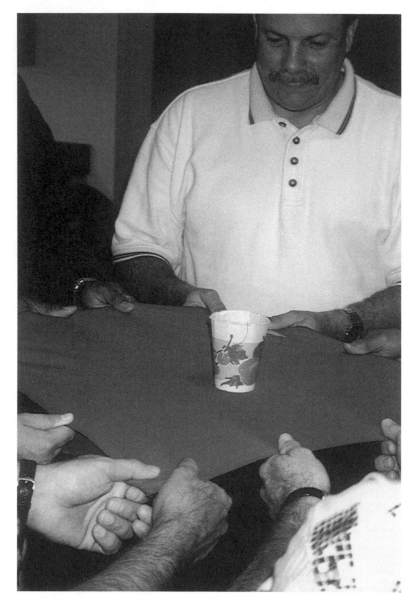

Water Fall

PROPS:
- One bandanna
- A plastic cup filled with water to within a 1/4 inch (6.4 mm) of the top or a cup filled with uncooked beans if you will be indoors (nobody likes to spill the beans)

OBJECTIVE:
A team holding a bandanna follows a leader around obstacles without spilling any water.

HISTORY:
At the beginning of 1995, I had an intern, Tim Reed, stay with me for a month. While we were planning for a group, he introduced me to this simple and powerful team building activity. Later, Joel Cryer was credited for teaching it to him.

INSTRUCTIONS:
(In groups of 3 to 8)

Take hold of your bandanna by the edges so that everyone has both hands on it. Pull it taught and make it flat.

I will place a cup of water in the middle of the bandanna. You may not let go of the bandanna and the edges of the bandanna must always be below the top of the cup. Without spilling any water or letting go of the bandanna, follow me.

Should you spill any of the water, we will start over.

FACILITATOR NOTES:
This activity demonstrates concepts such as systems thinking, cooperation, team coordination, trust, and problem solving

on the go.

Move slowly so that the group can keep up with you. This is not necessarily a race. Keep the obstacles fairly easy such as going through doorways, over railings, and around chairs. Tougher obstacles could be things like a stairway or under a table.

Finish the exercise by asking the team to place the bandanna and glass on the floor.

Obviously, you can make this activity easier or harder by how much water you put in the cup, by how narrow the cup's base is, and by the path you take.

Some teams will try to roll the bandanna toward the cup so they can hold it easier. I usually ask that the bandanna remain flat.

Work, Rest & Play Mate

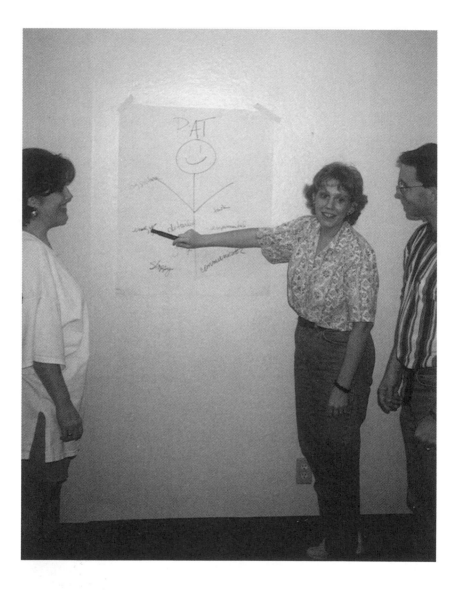

Work, Rest & Play Mate

PROPS:
None

OBJECTIVE:
The group will get to know two or three people better.

HISTORY:
I was preparing for a workshop to present to trainers when I realized we needed a creative introduction for people who had probably already done every creative introduction out there. As often happens, there was inspiration under pressure.

INSTRUCTIONS:
Divide the group into small groups of 3 or 4 people.

You will need to "create" another person to add to your small group who has a combination of the actual attributes in your small group. You will need to describe him or her in three areas: work, rest, and play.

If a person had the combination of the skills you have in your small group, what would he or she do for work? What things would he or she enjoy doing for leisure? Rest patterns? Be creative!

You have 6 minutes to discuss your person in the small groups and then up to 2 minutes to introduce your person to the rest of the group.

FACILITATOR NOTES:
Give everyone approximately 6 minutes in their small groups and then 2 minutes per presentation.

Sometimes people have a hard time combining their real experience and deciding what kind of job this person might have. I have found it useful to encourage them to make up a new occupation if needed.

Many people name their "person" with an androgynous name like Pat or Chris. It seems to add to the fun.

VARIATIONS:
Instead of asking the small groups to gather their real skills, leisure activities, and rest patterns, it can be interesting to ask them to pretend their "person" is a combination of their own fantasy lives.

Solutions (so far) and explanations

I = √T   the line is moved to form a square root symbol over a one, and the square root of one is one

I = \ ⁄I   a line is moved to form a multiplication symbol between two ones, one times one is one

I = \ I─I   a line is moved to form a subtraction symbol, two minus one is one

I = ▼I a line caps the "V" to form a triangular zero, zero one equals one

=N I I a line turns the "V" into an "N" to spell "nil" with the first two letters upper case and the last letter lower case, nil means nothing which is what is to the left of the equal sign

⁄=\ I I a line is moved to the left side to form an "X", "X" can equal anything including three

⌐ = V I I a line on the left is moved by bending it to form a seven, seven equals Roman number seven

|I =   II if the "V" is straightened, counted as one line, and moved to the left side of the equation, two equals two

✧✧✧✧✧✧✧✧✧✧✧✧✧✧✧✧✧✧✧✧✧✧✧✧✧✧✧✧✧✧✧✧

SIX a line in the shape of an "S" makes the puzzle spell six

IX6 a line in the shape of a "6" makes the puzzle six since one times six is six

—IX— straight line divides the puzzle so that it is a Roman numeral six if you look at it upside down with its mirror image below

IXI pretty sneaky, one straight line turns this into the expression of the absolute value of "X". . . which could be six

4X one bent line turns the one into a four, now using the rules of Roman numerals, the smaller number on the left is subtracted from the larger number on the right, ten minus Roman numeral four equals six

IIX this expression is defined as two parallel lines and four intersecting lines, add all the lines together and it's six

Secret instructions for Bolt In A Bottle:
The following description contains copious words for a fairly simple operation.
Overall concept:
Imagine taking a bolt or a screw and unrolling it. You would be left with slope or a ramp. If you put a ball on that slope, it would roll downhill. That is what happens to a bolt and a nut if they are vibrated. The nut rolls down the shaft of the bolt. If we did not have friction, the nut on <u>any</u> bolt would just spin

down the bolt because of the force of gravity. The solution to this puzzle gets you to overcome the friction between the nut and bolt by vibrating (tapping) them.

Taking it apart:
Hold the jar and dowel rod horizontal with the nut on the bottom side of the dowel rod. Tap on the rod and the nut should start slowly vibrating off the bolt.

Putting it back together:
Place the nut into the bottle. Make a strip of paper approximately one half inch wide and eight to eleven inches long. Poke the bolt through the paper at one end until the bolt can hang horizontally while you hold the other end of the paper. Lower the bolt into the bottle, then stick the dowel rod into the bottle. Carefully stick the bolt into the hole of the dowel rod and push it through the rod. (The paper is not absolutely necessary, but I find it easier than jockeying the bolt into the hole by chance.) Turn the bottle and the bolt so that the bottle is on its side and the bolt is pointing thread-end down. Shift the nut in the bottle so that the end of the bolt rests on the nut and the nut can screw onto the bolt. Carefully shake the dowel rod so that the nut and bolt barely screw together. Then gently turn the rod so that the nut is resting on top of the bolt end. Be careful not to let the bolt fall out of your dowel rod! Tap the dowel rod so that it vibrates and watch the nut slowly rotate down the shaft of the bolt. Once the nut has made a few rotations, you can get more rigorous with the tapping. Make sure the nut is not resting on the rod as you tap or you may unintentionally unscrew the nut.

. . . about Learning Unlimited Corporation

Imagine This:

"Good morning, Class! Today we are going to learn to ride a bicycle. After the 'How to Ride a Bicycle' video, we will be completing pages 24 - 48 of your workbook. A short break will be followed by small group discussions on the importance of riding bicycles. We will complete the training with an action planning process to transfer the skills you learn today into your job."

Learning to be a team is like learning to ride a bicycle.

Did you learn to ride a bicycle in a classroom???

Learning Unlimited Corporation puts work groups on the "teamwork" bicycle.

Learning Unlimited provides classroom concepts as the foundation for the real learning:
GROUPS BECOME TEAMS BY BEING TEAMS.

5155 East 51st, Suite 108
Tulsa, OK 74135

(888) 622-4203 toll free
(918) 622-3292
(918) 622-4203 fax

Experience-Based Training & Development

Assessment
All the training we provide is customized to the specific needs of the customer. Assessment is critical to creating a process that "fits". We strive to build upon effective training which has already occurred or provide proven training guides when the training concepts do not already exist. Surveys, interviews, in-house documents, business plans etc. all provide vital information to make our training "stick".

Customized Training
If you contacted all of our customers and asked them what they did in their training sessions, you would never hear the same schedule repeated. We are serious when we say the training is customized. We have designed programs for 30 minutes to 70 hours and for two to 3000 people at a time.

Follow-up and Evaluation
Follow-up sessions are scheduled with customers to provide ongoing support. Evaluation by means of pre- and post-assessments verifies the effectiveness of the training in terms of interpersonal and bottom line measures.

Consultation
We enjoy designing and implementing training. We also consult to the design of in-house training programs and organizational development.

The range of our training includes:

People Skills
- Effective Communication
- Negotiation
- Leadership Development
- Conflict Management
- Behavioral Styles
- Diversity
- Creativity
- Dealing with Change
- Trust
- Coaching
- Feedback

Task Skills
- Process Improvement
- Decision Making Tools
- Measurement
- Effective Meetings
- Goal Setting
- Strategic Planning
- Vision/Mission Creation

Trainer Skills
- Icebreakers
- Games & Initiatives
- Facilitator Training
- Training Design
- Ropes Course Facilitator Training
- Handling Difficult Situations

. . . about The Author

Sam has a Master's Degree in Industrial/Organizational Psychology from the University of Tulsa, and a Bachelor's Degree in Psychology from Texas Tech University in Lubbock.

Sam trains, facilitates, and speaks nationwide in a variety of corporate and educational settings including Fortune 500 companies, small businesses and universities. Best known for his creativity, Sam has trained groups of as few as two people and as many as three thousand. He certifies Ropes Course facilitators and develops related indoor and outdoor training activities for adults.

He is active in organizations such as the Association for Experiential Education, American Society for Training and Development, and the Tulsa Area Human Resources Association.

In 1996, Sam was recognized as "Practitioner of the Year" in a five-state region for his achievements in training by the Association for Experiential Education.

His other published materials include the *Feeding The Zircon Gorilla, 50 Ways To Use Your Noodle*, a *S.T.A.T.S. Test*, and *Indoor Games For College Students And The Extremely Bored*.

Ordering More Resources

Other Books:

Feeding The Zircon Gorilla
38 activities for teams
Full instructions and diagrams

50 Ways To Use Your Noodle
Games and problem solving activities using the foam pool noodles on dry land

Game Equipment for any of the activities within this book may be ordered directly

Workshops

"Bring the Activities to Life!"
"Experience them first-hand."

Schedule a workshop in your area.

Train your Staff and Train Yourself

Marbles Workshops
Activities from *Executive Marbles*

Gorilla Workshops
Activities from *Feeding The Zircon Gorilla*

Noodle Workshops
Activities from *50 Ways To Use Your Noodle*

• Train the Trainer style - Learn to facilitate the activities for your particular audience. Expect lots of ideas, hints, and variations.

Contact us for details

call - (918) 622-3292
(888) 622-4203 toll free
fax - (918) 622-4203
write - 5155 East 51st, Suite 108
Tulsa, OK 74135
e-mail - ssikes@npi.net
internet - www.learningunlimited.com

For those who want to know

Cover Design:
Jim Weems, AD GRAPHICS

Text and Layout:
Skia font
ClarisWorks 5.0
Macintosh PowerBook 1400cs

Photography:
Sam Sikes (with a lot of help and trust from
friends)

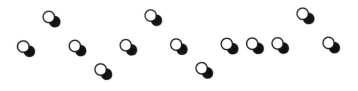